THE

ENCHANTED MOCCASINS

AND

OTHER LEGENDS

OF THE AMERICANS INDIANS

COMPILED FROM ORIGINAL SOURCES

BY

CORNELIUS MATTHEWS

WITH ILLUSTRATIONS

NEW YORK

G. P. PUTNAM'S SONS

182 FIFTH AVENUE

1877

AMS PRESS
NEW YORK

Reprinted from the edition of 1877, New York
First AMS EDITION published 1970
Manufactured in the United States of America

398.2
S372

International Standard Book Number: 0-404-04264-3

Library of Congress Card Catalog Number: 73-119646

AMS PRESS, INC.
NEW YORK, N.Y. 10003

PREFACE TO THE THIRD EDITION.

THE following stories have been, time out of mind, in
their original form, recited around the lodge-fires and
under the trees, by the Indian story-tellers, for the entertainment of the red children of the West. They were
originally compiled from the old tales and legends by
the late Henry R. Schoolcraft, and are now re-interpreted
and developed by the Editor, so as to enable them, as
far as worthy, to take a place with the popular versions
of the Arabian Nights' Entertainments, Cinderella,
Little Red Riding-hood, and other world-renowned
tales of Europe and the East, to which, in their original conception, they bear a resemblance in romantic
interest and quaint extravagance of fancy. The Editor
hopes that these beautiful legends of the West, if not
marred in the handling, will repay, in part, at least, the
glorious debt which we have incurred to the Eastern
World for her magical gifts of the same kind.

The reader is invited, in these stories, to look back
upon the Indian as he moved about the New World,
under the sky, along the streams, and through the forests, before he had the acquaintance, the companionship, or the enmity of the white man.

He lived in a world of nature, a world that, while familiar, never ceased to be for him strange, startling, and full of marvels; and the wonders that revealed themselves to his imagination took the shape of marvellous legends, which, like the legends of ancient Greece, were recited around the lodge-fires, until they became fixed in the minds of successive generations.

The Editor has, in this volume, attempted to present, in a form adapted to the comprehension and sympathy of the readers of to-day, a selection of some of the most striking and characteristic of these legends.

It is hoped that they will not only prove attractive to the principal readers of fairy tales, the boys and girls, but will also be found of interest and value to the student of aboriginal ways of life and of thought, and to those who appreciate the importance in the history of man of the study of primitive folk-lore.

The original edition of the work was published in 1867, under the title of "The Indian Fairy Book," and has been for some years out of print.

In response to continued demand, this edition is now issued, in more attractive form, and under a somewhat modified and more appropriate title.

C. M.

New York, Sept., 1877.

CONTENTS.

———◆◆◆———

ILLUSTRATIONS.

I.

THE CELESTIAL SISTERS.

WAUPEE, or the White Hawk, lived in a remote part of the forest, where animals abounded. Every day he returned from the chase with a large spoil, for he was one of the most skillful and lucky hunters of his tribe. His form was like the cedar; the fire of youth beamed from his eye; there was no forest too gloomy for him to penetrate, and no track made by bird or beast of any kind which he could not readily follow.

One day he had gone beyond any point which he had ever before visited. He traveled through an open wood, which enabled him to see a great distance. At length he beheld a light breaking through the foliage of the distant trees, which made him sure that he was on the borders of a prairie. It was a wide plain, covered with long blue grass, and enameled with flowers of a thousand lovely tints.

After walking for some time without a path, musing upon the open country, and enjoying the fragrant breeze, he suddenly came to a ring worn among the grass and the flowers, as if it had been made by footsteps moving lightly round and round. But it was strange—so strange as to cause the White Hawk to pause and gaze long and fixedly upon the ground—there was no path which led to this flowery circle. There was not even a crushed leaf nor a broken twig, nor the least trace of a footstep, approaching or retiring, to be found. He thought he would hide himself and lie in wait to discover, if he could, what this strange circle meant.

Presently he heard the faint sounds of music in the air. He looked up in the direction they came from, and as the magic notes died away he saw a small object, like a little summer cloud that approaches the earth, floating down from above. At first it was very small, and seemed as if it could have been blown away by the first breeze that came along; but it rapidly grew as he gazed upon it, and the music every moment came clearer and more sweetly to his ear. As it neared the earth it appeared as a basket, and it was filled with twelve sisters, of the most lovely forms and enchanting beauty.

As soon as the basket touched the ground they leaped out, and began straightway to dance, in the most joyous manner, around the magic ring, striking, as they did so, a shining ball, which uttered the most ravishing melodies, and kept time as they danced

The White Hawk, from his concealment, entranced, gazed upon their graceful forms and movements. He admired them all, but he was most pleased with the youngest. He longed to be at her side, to embrace her, to call her his own; and unable to remain longer a silent admirer, he rushed out and endeavored to seize this twelfth beauty who so enchanted him. But the sisters, with the quickness of birds, the moment they descried the form of a man, leaped back into the basket, and were drawn up into the sky.

Lamenting his ill-luck, Waupee gazed longingly upon the fairy basket as it ascended and bore the lovely sisters from his view. "They are gone," he said, " and I shall see them no more."

He returned to his solitary lodge, but he found no relief to his mind. He walked abroad, but to look at the sky, which had withdrawn from his sight the only being he had ever loved, was painful to him now.

The next day, selecting the same hour, the White Hawk went back to the prairie, and took his station near the ring; in order to deceive the sisters, he assumed the form of an opossum, and sat among the grass as if he were there engaged in chewing the cud. He had not waited long when he saw the cloudy basket descend, and heard the same sweet music falling as before. He crept slowly toward the ring; but the instant the sisters caught sight of him they were startled, and sprang into their car. It rose a short distance when one of the elder sisters spoke:

"Perhaps," she said, "it is come to show us how the game is played by mortals."

"Oh no," the youngest replied; "quick, let us ascend."

And all joining in a chant, they rose out of sight.

Waupee, casting off his disguise, walked sorrowfully back to his lodge—but ah, the night seemed very long to lonely White Hawk! His whole soul was filled with the thought of the beautiful sister.

Betimes, the next day, he returned to the haunted spot, hoping and fearing, and sighing as though his very soul would leave his body in its anguish. He reflected upon the plan he should follow to secure success. He had already failed twice; to fail a third time would be fatal. Near by he found an old stump, much covered with moss, and just then in use as the residence of a number of mice, who had stopped there on a pilgrimage to some relatives on the other side of the prairie. The White Hawk was so pleased with their tidy little forms that he thought he, too, would be a mouse, especially as they were by no means formidable to look at, and would not be at all likely to create alarm.

He accordingly, having first brought the stump and set it near the ring, without further notice became a mouse, and peeped and sported about, and kept his sharp little eyes busy with the others; but he did not forget to keep one eye up toward the sky, and one ear wide open in the same direction.

It was not long before the sisters, at their customary hour, came down and resumed their sport.

"But see," cried the younger sister, "that stump was not there before."

She ran off, frightened, toward the basket. Her sisters only smiled, and gathering round the old tree-stump, they struck it, in jest, when out ran the mice, and among them Waupee. They killed them all but one, which was pursued by the younger sister. Just as she had raised a silver stick which she held in her hand to put an end to it, too, the form of the White Hawk arose, and he clasped his prize in his arms. The other eleven sprang to their basket, and were drawn up to the skies.

Waupee exerted all his skill to please his bride and win her affections. He wiped the tears from her eyes; he related his adventures in the chase; he dwelt upon the charms of life on the earth. He was constant in his attentions, keeping fondly by her side, and picking out the way for her to walk as he led her gently toward his lodge. He felt his heart glow with joy as he entered it, and from that moment he was one of the happiest of men.

Winter and summer passed rapidly away, and as the spring drew near with its balmy gales and its many-colored flowers, their happiness was increased by the presence of a beautiful boy in their lodge. What more of earthly blessing was there for them to enjoy?

Waupee's wife was a daughter of one of the stars; and as the scenes of earth began to pall upon her sight, she sighed to revisit her father. But she was obliged to hide these feelings from her husband. She remembered the charm that would carry her up, and while White Hawk was engaged in the chase, she took occasion to construct a wicker basket, which she kept concealed. In the mean time, she collected such rarities from the earth as she thought would please her father, as well as the most dainty kinds of food.

One day when Waupee was absent, and all was in readiness, she went out to the charmed ring, taking with her her little son. As they entered the car she commenced her magical song, and the basket rose. The song was sad, and of a lowly and mournful cadence, and as it was wafted far away by the wind, it caught her husband's ear. It was a voice which he well knew, and he instantly ran to the prairie.

Though he made breathless speed, he could not reach the ring before his wife and child had ascended beyond his reach. He lifted up his voice in loud appeals, but they were unavailing. The basket still went up. He watched it till it became a small speck, and finally it vanished in the sky. He then bent his head down to the ground, and was miserable.

Through a long winter and a long summer Waupee bewailed his loss, but he found no relief. The beautiful spirit had come and gone, and he should see it no more!

He mourned his wife's loss sorely. but his son's still more; for the boy had both the mother's beauty and the father's strength.

In the mean time his wife had reached her home in the stars, and in the blissful employments of her father's house she had almost forgotten that she had left a husband upon the earth. But her son, as he grew up, resembled more and more his father, and every day he was restless and anxious to visit the scene of his birth. His grandfather said to his daughter, one day:

" Go, my child, and take your son down to his father, and ask him to come up and live with us. But tell him to bring along a specimen of each kind of bird and animal he kills in the chase."

She accordingly took the boy and descended.

The White Hawk, who was ever near the enchanted spot, heard her voice as she came down the sky. His heart beat with impatience as he saw her form and that of his son, and they were soon clasped in his arms.

He heard the message of the Star, and he began to hunt with the greatest activity, that he might collect the present with all dispatch. He spent whole nights, as well as days, in searching for every curious and beautiful animal and bird. He only preserved a foot, a wing, or a tail of each.

When all was ready, Waupee visited once more each favorite spot—the hill-top whence he had been used to see the rising sun; the stream where he had sported as a boy; the old lodge, now looking sad and solemn, which he was to sit in no more; and last of all, coming to the magic circle, he gazed widely around him with tearful eyes, and, taking his wife and child by the hand, they entered the car and were drawn up—into a country far beyond the flight of birds, or the power of mortal eye to pierce.

Great joy was manifested upon their arrival at the starry plains. The Star Chief invited all his people to a feast; and when they had assembled, he proclaimed aloud that each one might continue as he was, an inhabitant of his own dominions, or select of the earthly gifts such as he liked best. A very strange confusion immediately arose; not one but sprang forward. Some chose a foot, some a wing, some a tail, and some a claw. Those who selected tails or claws were changed into animals, and ran off; the others assumed the form of birds, and flew away. Waupee chose a white hawk's feather. His wife and son followed his example, and each one became a white hawk. He spread his wings, and, followed by his wife and son, descended with the other birds to the earth, where he is still to be found, with the brightness of the starry plains in his eye, and the freedom of the heavenly breezes in his wings.

II.

THE BOY WHO SET A SNARE FOR THE SUN.

AT the time when the animals reigned in the earth, they had killed all the people but a girl and her little brother, and these two were living in fear, in an out-of-the-way place. The boy was a perfect little pigmy, and never grew beyond the size of a mere infant; but the girl increased with her years, so that the task of providing food and shelter fell wholly upon her. She went out daily to get wood for the lodge-fire, and she took her little brother with her that no mishap might befall him; for he was too little to leave alone. A big bird, of a mischievous disposition, might have flown away with him. She made him a bow and arrows, and said to him one day, "My little brother, I will leave you behind where I have been gathering the wood; you must hide yourself, and you will soon see the snow-birds come and pick the worms out of the logs which I have piled up. Shoot one of them and bring it home."

He obeyed her, and tried his best to kill one, but he came home unsuccessful. His sister told him that he must not despair, but try again the next day.

She accordingly left him at the gathering-place of the wood, and returned to the lodge. Toward nightfall she heard his little footsteps crackling through the snow, and he hurried in and threw down, with an air of triumph, one of the birds which he had killed. "My sister," said he, "I wish you to skin it, and stretch the skin, and when I have killed more, I will have a coat made out of them."

"But what shall we do with the body?" said she; for they had always up to that time lived upon greens and berries.

"Cut it in two," he answered, "and season our pottage with one half of it at a time."

It was their first dish of game, and they relished it greatly.

The boy kept on in his efforts, and in the course of time he killed ten birds—out of the skins of which his sister made him a little coat: being very small, he had a very pretty coat, and a bird skin to spare.

"Sister," said he, one day, as he paraded up and down before the lodge, enjoying his new coat, and fancifying himself the greatest little fellow in the world—as he was, for there was no other beside him— "My sister, are we really alone in the world, or are

we playing at it ?   Is there nobody else living ?
And, tell me, was all this great broad earth and this
huge big sky made for a little boy and girl like you
and me ?"

She told him, by no means ;   there were many
folks very unlike a harmless girl and boy, such as
they were, who lived in a certain other quarter of the
earth, who had killed off all of their kinsfolk ; and
that if he would live blameless and not endanger his
life, he must never go where they were.   This only
served to inflame the boy's curiosity ; and he soon
after took his bow and arrows and went in that
direction.   After walking a long time and meeting
no one, he became tired, and stretched himself upon
a high green knoll where the day's warmth had
melted off the snow.

It was a charming place to lie upon, and he fell
asleep ; and, while sleeping, the sun beat so hot upon
him that it not only singed his bird-skin coat, but it
so shrivelled and shrunk and tightened it upon the
little boy's body, as to wake him up.

When he felt how the sun had seared and the mischief its fiery beams had played with the coat he was
so proud of, he flew into a great passion, and berated
the sun in a terrible way for a little boy no higher
than a man's knee, and he vowed fearful things
against it.

"Do not think you are too high," said he ; " I

shall revenge myself. Oh, sun! I will have you for
a plaything yet."

On coming home he gave an account of his misfortune to his sister, and bitterly bewailed the spoiling
of his new coat. He would not eat—not so much as
a single berry. He lay down as one that fasts; nor
did he move nor change his manner of lying for ten
full days, though his sister strove to prevail on him
to rise. At the end of ten days he turned over, and
then he lay full ten days on the other side.

When he got up he was very pale, but very resolute too. He bade his sister make a snare, for, he
informed her, that he meant to catch the sun. She
said she had nothing; but after awhile she brought
forward a deer's sinew which the father had left, and
which she soon made into a string suitable for a
noose. The moment she showed it to him he was
quite wroth, and told her that would not do, and
directed her to find something else. She said she
had nothing—nothing at all. At last she thought of
the bird-skin that was left over when the coat was
made; and this she wrought into a string. With this
the little boy was more vexed than before. "The
sun has had enough of my bird-skins," he said; "find
something else." She went out of the lodge saying
to herself, "Was there ever so obstinate a boy?" She
did not dare to answer this time that she had nothing. Luckily she thought of her own beautiful hair,

and pulling some of it from among her locks, she quickly braided it into a cord, and, returning, she handed it to her brother. The moment his eye fell upon this jet black braid he was delighted. " This will do," he said ; and he immediately began to run it back and forth through his hands as swiftly as he could ; and as he drew it forth, he tried its strength. He said again, " this will do ;" and winding it in a glossy coil about his shoulders, he set out a little after midnight. His object was to catch the sun before he rose. He fixed his snare firmly on a spot just where the sun must strike the land as it rose above the earth ; and sure enough, he caught the sun, so that it was held fast in the cord and did not rise.

The animals who ruled the earth were immediately put into great commotion. They had no light ; and they ran to and fro, calling out to each other, and in-quiring what had happened. They summoned a council to debate upon the matter, and an old dor-mouse, suspecting where the trouble lay, proposed that some one should be appointed to go and cut the cord. This was a bold thing to undertake, as the rays of the sun could not fail to burn whoever should venture so near to them.

At last the venerable dormouse himself undertook it, for the very good reason that no one else would. At this time the dormouse was the largest animal in the world. When he stood up he looked like a mountain. It made haste to the place where the sun lay ensnared, and as it came nearer and nearer, its back began to smoke and burn with the heat, and the whole top of his huge bulk was turned in a very short time to enormous heaps of ashes. It succeeded, however, in cutting the cord with its teeth and freeing the sun, which rolled up again, as round and beautiful as ever, into the wide blue sky. But the dormouse—or blind woman as it is called—was shrunk away to a very small size ; and that is the reason why it is now one of the tiniest creatures upon the earth.

The little boy returned home when he discovered that the sun had escaped his snare, and devoted himself entirely to hunting. "If the beautiful hair of my sister would not hold the sun fast, nothing in the world could," he said. "He was not born, a little fellow like himself, to look after the sun. It required one greater and wiser than he was to regulate that." And he went out and shot ten more snow-birds ; for in this business he was very expert ; and he had a new bird-skin coat made, which was prettier than the one he had worn before.

III.

STRONG DESIRE, AND THE RED SORCERER.

THERE was a man called Odshedoph, or the Child of Strong Desires, who had a wife and one son. He had withdrawn his family from the village, where they had spent the winter, to the neighborhood of a distant forest, where game abounded. This wood was a day's travel from his winter home, and under its ample shadow the wife fixed the lodge, while the husband went out to hunt. Early in the evening he returned with a deer, and, being weary and athirst, he asked his son, whom he called Strong Desire, to go to the river for some water. The son replied that it was dark, and he was afraid. His father still urged him, saying that his mother, as well as himself, was tired, and the distance to the water very short. But no persuasion could overcome the young man's reluctance. He refused to go.

"Ah, my son," said the father, at last, "if you

are afraid to go to the river, you will never kill the Red Head."

The stripling was deeply vexed by this observation; it seemed to touch him to the very quick. He mused in silence. He refused to eat, and made no reply when spoken to. He sat by the lodge door all the night through, looking up at the stars, and sighing like one sorely distressed.

The next day he asked his mother to dress the skin of the deer, and to make it into moccasins for him, while he busied himself in preparing a bow and arrows.

As soon as these were in readiness, he left the lodge one morning, at sunrise, without saying a word to his father or mother. As he passed along, he fired one of his arrows into the air, which fell westward. He took that course, and coming to the spot where the arrow had fallen, he was rejoiced to find it piercing the heart of a deer. He refreshed himself with a meal of the venison, and the next morning he fired another arrow. Following its course, after traveling all day he found that he had transfixed another deer. In this manner he fired four arrows, and every evening he discovered that he had killed a deer.

By a strange oversight, he left the arrows sticking in the carcasses, and passed on without withdrawing them Having in this way no arrow for the fifth

day, he was in great distress at night for the want
of food.

At last he threw himself upon the earth in despair, concluding that he might as well perish there
as go further. But he had not lain long before he
heard a hollow rumbling noise, in the ground beneath
him, like that of an earthquake moving slowly along.

He sprang up, and discovered at a distance the
figure of a human being, walking with a stick. He
looked attentively, and saw that the figure was walking in a wide beaten path in a prairie, leading from
a dusky lodge to a lake, whose waters were black and
turbid.

To his surprise, this lodge, which had not been in
view when he cast himself upon the ground, was
now near at hand. He approached a little nearer,
and concealed himself; and in a moment he discovered that the figure was no other than that of the
terrible witch, the little old woman who makes war.
Her path to the lake was perfectly smooth and solid,
and the noise Strong Desire had heard was caused
by the striking of her walking staff upon the ground.
The top of this staff was decorated with a string of
the toes and bills of birds of every kind, who, at
every stroke of the stick, fluttered and sung their various notes in concert.

She entered her lodge and laid off her mantle,
which was entirely composed of the scalps of women.

Before folding it, she shook it several times, and at every shake the scalps uttered loud shouts of laughter, in which the old hag joined. The boy, who lingered at the door, was greatly alarmed, but he uttered no cry.

After laying by the cloak, she came directly to him. Looking at him steadily, she informed him that she had known him from the time he had left his father's lodge, and had watched his movements. She told him not to fear or despair, for she would be his protector and friend. She invited him into her lodge, and gave him a supper. During the repast, she questioned him as to his motives for visiting her. He related his history, stated the manner in which he had been disgraced, and the difficulties he labored under.

" Now tell me truly," said the little old woman who makes war, " you were afraid to go to the water in the dark."

" I was," Strong Desire answered, promptly.

As he replied, the hag waved her staff. The birds set up a clamorous cry, and the mantle shook violently as all the scalps burst into a hideous shout of laughter.

" And are you afraid now," she asked again.

" I am," again answered Strong Desire, without hesitation.

" But you are not afraid to speak the truth," re-

2

joined the little old woman. " You will be a brave man yet."

She cheered him with the assurance of her friendship, and began at once to exercise her power upon him. His hair being very short, she took a great leaden comb, and after drawing it through his locks several times, they became of a handsome length like those of a beautiful young woman. She then proceeded to dress him as a female, furnishing him with the necessary garments, and tinting his face with colors of the most charming dye. She gave him, too, a bowl of shining metal. She directed him to put in his girdle a blade of scented sword-grass, and to proceed the next morning to the banks of the lake, which was no other than that over which the Red Head reigned. Now Hah-Undo-Tah, or the Red Head, was a most powerful sorcerer, living upon an island in the centre of his realm of water, and he was the terror of all the country. She informed him that there would be many Indians upon the island, who, as soon as they saw him use the shining bowl to drink with, would come and solicit him to be their wife, and to take him over to the island. These offers he was to refuse, and to say that he had come a great distance to be the wife of the Red Head, and that if the chief could not seek her for himself, she would return to her village. She said, that as soon as the Red Head heard of this he would come for her in his own canoe, in which she must embark.

"On reaching the shore," added the little old woman, "you must consent to be his wife ; and in the evening you are to induce him to take a walk out of the village, and when you have reached a lonesome spot, use the first opportunity to cut off his head with the blade of grass."

She also gave Strong Desire general advice how he was to conduct himself to sustain his assumed character of a woman. His fear would scarcely permit him to consent to engage in an adventure attended with so much danger ; but the recollection of his father's looks and reproaches of the want of courage, decided him.

Early in the morning he left the lodge of the little old woman who makes war, which was clouded in a heavy brackish fog, so thick and heavy to breathe, that he with difficulty made his way forth. When he turned to look back for it, it was gone.

He took the hard beaten path to the banks of the lake, and made for the water at a point directly opposite the Red Head's lodge.

Where he now stood it was beautiful day. The heavens were clear, and the sun shone out as brightly to Strong Desire as on the first morning when he had put forth his little head from the door of his father's lodge. He had not been long there, saunter-

ing along the beach, when he displayed the glittering bowl by dipping water from the lake. Very soon
a number of canoes came off from the island. The
men admired his dress, and were charmed with his
beauty, and almost with one voice they all made proposals of marriage. These, Strong Desire promptly
declined.

When this was reported to Red Head, he ordered
his royal bark to be launched by his chosen men of
the oar, and crossed over to see this wonderful girl.
As they approached the shore, Strong Desire saw
that the ribs of the sorcerer's canoe were formed of
living rattlesnakes, whose heads pointed outward to
guard him from his enemies. Being invited, he
had no sooner stepped into the canoe, than they began to hiss and rattle furiously, which put him in a
great fright; but the magician spoke to them, when
they became pacified and quiet. Shortly after they
were at the landing upon the island. The marriage
took place immediately; and the bride made presents of various valuables which had been furnished
her by the old witch who inhabited the cloudy lodge.

As they were sitting in the lodge, surrounded by
the friends and relatives, the mother of the Red
Head regarded the face of her new daughter-in-law
for a long time with fixed attention. From this
scrutiny she was convinced that this singular and
hasty marriage boded no good to her son. She drew

him aside, and disclosed to him her suspicions.
This can be no female, said she ; she has the figure and manners, the countenance, and more especially the eyes, are beyond a doubt those of a man.
Her husband rejected her suspicions, and rebuked
her severely for entertaining such notions of her own
daughter-in-law. She still urged her doubts, which
so vexed the husband that he broke his pipe-stem
in her face, and called her an owl.

This act astonished the company, who sought an
explanation ; and it was no sooner given, than the
mock bride, rising with an air of offended dignity,
informed the Red Head that after receiving so gross
an affront from his relatives she could not think of
remaining with him as his wife, but should forthwith
return to her own friends.

With a toss of the head, like that of an angry
female, Strong Desire left the lodge, followed by Red
Head, and walked away until he came to the beach
of the island, near the spot where they had first
landed. Red Head entreated him to remain, urging
every motive, and making all sorts of magnificent
promises—none of which seemed to make the least
impression. Strong Desire, Red Head thought, was
very hard-hearted. During these appeals they had
seated themselves upon the ground, and Red Head,
in great affliction, reclined his head upon his fancied
wife's lap. Strong Desire now changed his manner

was very kind and soothing, and suggested in the
most winning accent that if Red Head would sleep
soundly for awhile he might possibly dream himself
out of all his troubles. Red Head, delighted at so
happy a prospect, said that he would fall asleep immediately.

"You have killed a good many men in your time,
Red Head," said Strong Desire, by way of suggest-
ing an agreeable train of ideas to the sorcerer.

"Hundreds," answered Red Head; "and what is
better, now that I am fairly settled in life by this
happy marriage, I shall be able to give my whole attention to massacre."

"And you will kill hundreds more," interposed
Strong Desire, in the most insinuating manner im-
aginable.

"Just so, my dear," Red Head replied, with a
great leer; "thousands. There will be no end to my
delicious murders. I love dearly to kill people. I
would like to kill you if you were not my wife."

"There, there," said Strong Desire, with the coax-
ing air of a little coquette, "go to sleep; that's a
good Red Head."

No other subject of conversation occurring to the
chief, now that he had exhausted the delightful topic
of wholesale murder, he straightway fell into a deep
sleep.

The chance so anxiously sought for had come; and

Strong Desire, with a smiling eye, drawing his blade of grass with lightning swiftness once across the neck of the Red Head, severed the huge and wicked head from the body.

In a moment, stripping off his woman's dress, underneath which he had all along worn his male attire, Strong Desire seized the bleeding trophy, plunged into the lake, and swam safely over to the main shore. He had scarcely reached it, when, looking back, he saw amid the darkness the torches of persons come out in search of the new married couple. He listened until they had found the headless body, and he heard their piercing shrieks of rage and sorrow as he took his way to the lodge of his kind adviser.

The little old woman who makes war was in an excellent humor, and she received Strong Desire with rejoicing. She admired his prudence, and assured him his bravery should never be questioned again. Lifting up the head, which she gazed upon with vast delight, she said he need only have brought the scalp. Cutting off a lock of the hair for herself, she told him he might now return with the head, which would be evidence of an achievement that would cause his own people to respect him.

"In your way home," added the little old woman, "you will meet with but one difficulty. Maunkahkeesh, the Spirit of the Earth, requires an offering or sacrifice from all of her sons who perform extraordinary deeds. As you walk along in a prairie there will be an earthquake; the earth will open and divide the prairie in the middle. Take this partridge and throw it into the opening, and instantly spring over it."

With many thanks to the little old witch, who had so faithfully befriended him, Strong Desire took leave of her, and having, by the course pointed out, safely passed the earthquake, he arrived near his own village. He secretly hid his precious trophy.

On entering the village, he found that his parents had returned from the place of their spring encampment by the wood-side, and that they were in heavy sorrowing for their son, whom they supposed to be lost. One and another of the young men had presented themselves to the disconsolate parents, and said, " Look up, I am your son ;" but when they looked up, they beheld not the familiar face of Strong Desire.

Having been often deceived in this manner, when their own son in truth presented himself they sat with their heads down, and with their eyes nearly blinded with weeping. It was some time before they could be prevailed upon to bestow a glance upon him. It was still longer before they could recognize him as their son who had refused to draw water from the river, at night, for fear, for his countenance was no longer that of a timid stripling; it was that of a man who has seen and done great things, and who has the heart to do greater still.

When he recounted his adventures they believed him mad. The young men laughed at him—him, Strong Desire—who feared to walk to the river at night-time.

He left the lodge, and ere their laughter had ceased, returned with his trophy. He held aloft the head of the Red Sorcerer, with the great ghastly leer which lighted it up before his last sleep, at prospect of a thousand future murders, fresh upon it. It was easily recognized, and the young men who had scoffed at Strong Desire shrunk into the corners out of sight. Strong Desire had conquered the terrible Red Head! All doubts of the truth of his adventures were dispelled.

He was greeted with joy, and placed among the first warriors of the nation. He finally became a chief, and his family were ever after respected and esteemed.

2*

IV.

THE WONDERFUL EXPLOITS OF GRASSHOPPER.

A MAN, of small stature, found himself standing alone on a prairie. He thought to himself, " How came I here ? Are there no beings on this earth but myself ? I must travel and see. I must walk till I find the abodes of men."

So soon as his mind was made up, he set out, he knew not whither, in search of habitations. He was a resolute little fellow, and no difficulties could turn him from his purpose : neither prairies, rivers, woods nor storms, had the effect to daunt his courage or turn him back. After traveling a long time, he came to a wood, in which he saw decayed stumps of trees, as if they had been cut in ancient times, but no other trace of men. Pursuing his journey, he found more recent marks of the same kind ; after this, he came upon fresh traces of human beings ; first their footsteps, and then the wood they had felled, lying in heaps. Pushing on, he emerged toward dusk from the forest, and beheld at a distance a large village of high lodges standing on rising ground.

"I am tired of this dog-trot," he said to himself. "I will arrive there on a run."

He started off with all his speed. On coming to the first lodge, without any especial exertion, he jumped over it, and found himself standing by the door on the other side. Those within saw something pass over the opening in the roof; they thought from the shadow it cast that it must have been some huge bird—and then they heard a thump upon the ground. "What is that?" they all said and several ran out to see.

They invited him in, and he found himself in company with an old chief and several men who were seated in the lodge. Meat was set before him; after which the old chief asked him whither he was going, and what was his name. He answered that he was in search of adventures, and that his name was "Grasshopper."

They all opened their eyes upon the stranger with a broad stare.

"Grasshopper!" whispered one to another; and a general titter went round.

They invited him to stay with them, which he was inclined to do; for it was a pleasant village, but so small as to constantly embarrass Grasshopper. He was in perpetual trouble; whenever he shook hands

with a stranger, to whom he might be introduced,
such was the abundance of his strength, without
meaning it, he wrung his arm off at the shoulder.
Once or twice, in mere sport, he cuffed the boys,
about the lodge, by the side of the head, and they
flew out of sight as though they had been shot from
a bow ; nor could they ever be found again, though
they were searched for in all the country round, far
and wide. If Grasshopper proposed to himself a
short stroll in the morning, he was at once miles
out of town. When he entered a lodge, if he happened for a moment to forget himself, he walked
straight through the leathern, or wooden, or earthen
walls, as if he had been merely passing through a
bush. At his meals he broke in pieces all the
dishes, set them down as lightly as he would ; and
putting a leg out of bed when he rose, it was a
common thing for him to push off the top of the
lodge.

He wanted more elbow-room ; and after a short
stay, in which, by the accidentally letting go of his
strength, he had nearly laid waste the whole place,
and filled it with demolished lodges and broken pot-
tery, and one-armed men, he made up his mind to go
further, taking with him a young man who had
formed a strong attachment for him, and who might
serve him as his pipe-bearer ; for Grasshopper was a
huge smoker, and vast clouds followed him wherever

he went ; so that people could say, "Grasshopper is coming !" by the mighty smoke he raised.

They set out together, and when his companion was fatigued with walking, Grasshopper would put him forward on his journey a mile or two by giving him a cast in the air, and lighting him in a soft place among the trees, or in a cool spot in a water-pond, among the sedges and water-lilies. At other times he would lighten the way by showing off a few tricks, such as leaping over trees, and turning round on one leg till he made the dust fly ; at which the pipe-bearer was mightily pleased, although it sometimes happened that the character of these gambols frightened him. For Grasshopper would, without the least hint of such an intention, jump into the air far ahead, and it would cost the little pipe-bearer half a day's hard travel to come up with him ; and then the dust Grasshopper raised was often so thick and heavy as to completely bury the poor little pipe-bearer, and compel Grasshopper to dig diligently and with might and main to get him out alive.

One day they came to a very large village, where they were well received. After staying in it some time (in the course of which Grasshopper, in a fit of abstraction, walked straight through the sides of three lodges without stopping to look for the door), they were informed of a number of wicked spirits, who lived at a distance, and who made it a practice to kill all who came to their lodge. Attempts had been made to destroy them, but they had always proved more than a match for such as had come out against them.

Grasshopper determined to pay them a visit, although he was strongly advised not to do so. The chief of the village warned him of the great danger he would incur, but finding Grasshopper resolved, he said:

"Well, if you will go, being my guest, I will send twenty warriors to serve you."

Grasshopper thanked him for the offer, although he suggested that he thought he could get along without them, at which the little pipe-bearer grinned, for his master had never shown in that village what he could do, and the chief thought that Grasshopper, being little himself, would be likely to need twenty warriors, at the least, to encounter the wicked spirits with any chance of success. Twenty young men made their appearance. They set forward, and after about a day's journey they descried the lodge of the Manitoes.

Grasshopper placed his friend, the pipe-bearer, and the warriors, near enough to see all that passed, while he went alone to the lodge.

As he entered, Grasshopper saw five horrid-looking Manitoes in the act of eating. It was the father and his four sons. They were really hideous to look upon. Their eyes were swimming low in their heads, and they glared about as if they were half starved. They offered Grasshopper something to eat, which he politely refused, for he had a strong suspicion that it was the thigh-bone of a man.

"What have you come for?" said the old one.

"Nothing," answered Grasshopper; "where is your uncle?"

They all stared at him, and answered:

"We ate him, yesterday. What do you want?"

"Nothing," said Grasshopper; "where is your grandfather?'

They all answered, with another broad stare:

"We ate him a week ago. Do you not wish to wrestle?"

"Yes," replied Grasshopper, "I don't mind if I do take a turn; but you must be easy with me, for you see I am very little."

Pipe-bearer, who stood near enough to overhear the conversation, grinned from ear to ear when he caught this remark. The Manitoes answered:

"Oh yes, we will be easy with you."

And as they said this they looked at each other, and rolled their eyes about in a dreadful manner. A hideous smile came over their faces as they whispered among themselves:

"It's a pity he's so thin. You go," they said to the eldest brother.

The two got ready—the Manito and Grasshopper
—and they were soon clinched in each other's arms
for a deadly throw. Grasshopper knew their object
—his death; they wanted a taste of his delicate
little body, and he was determined they should
have it, perhaps in a different sense from that they
intended.

"Haw! haw!" they cried, and soon the dust and
dry leaves flew about as if driven by a strong wind.
The Manito was strong, but Grasshopper thought he
could master him; and all at once giving him a sly
trip, as the wicked spirit was trying to finish his
breakfast with a piece out of his shoulder, he sent
the Manito head-foremost against a stone; and, calling aloud to the three others, he bade them come and
take the body away.

The brothers now stepped forth in quick succession,
but Grasshopper having got his blood up, and lim-
bered himself by exercise, soon dispatched the three
—sending one this way, another that, and the third
straight up into the air, so high that he never came
down again.

It was time for the old Manito to be frightened,
and dreadfully frightened he got, and ran for his
life, which was the very worst thing he could have
done; for Grasshopper, of all his gifts of strength,
was most noted for his speed of foot. The old Manito set off, and for mere sport's sake, Grasshopper

pursued him. Sometimes he was before the wicked
old spirit, sometimes he was flying over his head,
and then he would keep along at a steady trot just
at his heels, till he had blown all the breath out of
the old knave's body.

Meantime his friend, the pipe-bearer, and the
twenty young warriors, cried out:

" Ha, ha, ah! ha, ha, ah! Grasshopper is driving
him before him!"

The Manito only turned his head now and then to
look back. At length, when he was tired of the
sport, to be rid of him, Grasshopper, with a gentle
application of his foot, sent the wicked old Manito
whirling away through the air, in which he made a
great number of the most curious turn-overs in the
world, till he came to alight, when it so happened
that he fell astride of an old bull-buffalo, grazing in
a distant pasture, who straightway set off with him
at a long gallop, and the old Manito has not been
heard of to this day.

The warriors and the pipe-bearer and Grasshopper
set to work and burned down the lodge of the wicked
spirits, and then when they came to look about, they
saw that the ground was strewn on all sides with
human bones bleaching in the sun ; these were the
unhappy victims of the Manitoes. Grasshopper then
took three arrows from his girdle, and after having
performed a ceremony to the Great Spirit, he shot

one into the air, crying, "You are lying down ; rise up, or you will be hit !"

The bones all moved to one place. He shot the second arrow, repeating the same words, when each bone drew toward its fellow-bone ; the third arrow brought forth to life the whole multitude of people who had been killed by the Manitoes. Grasshopper conducted the crowd to the chief of the village, who had proved his friend, and gave them into his hands. The chief was there with his counselors, to whom he spoke apart.

"Who is more worthy," said the chief to Grass-hopper, "to rule than you. *You* alone can defend them."

Grasshopper thanked him, and told him that he was in search of more adventures. "I have done some things," said little Grasshopper, rather boast-fully, "and I think I can do some more."

The chief still urged him, but he was eager to go, and naming pipe-bearer to tarry and take his place, he set out again on his travels, promising that he would some time or other come back and see them.

"Ho ! ho ! ho !" they all cried. "Come back again and see us !" He renewed his promise that he would ; and then set out alone.

After traveling some time he came to a great lake, and on looking about he discovered a very large otter on an island. He thought to himself, "His skin will

make me a fine pouch." And he immediately drew
up at long shots, and drove an arrow into his side.
He waded into the lake, and with some difficulty
dragged him ashore, and up a hill overlooking the
lake.

As soon as Grasshopper got the otter into the sunshine where it was warm, he skinned him, and threw
the carcass some distance off, thinking the war-eagle
would come, and that he should have a chance to
secure his feathers as ornaments for the head ; for
Grasshopper began to be proud, and was disposed to
display himself.

He soon heard a rushing noise as of a loud wind,
but could see nothing. Presently a large eagle dropped, as if from the air, upon the otter's carcass.
Grasshopper drew his bow, and the arrow passed
through under both of his wings. The bird made a
convulsive flight upward, with such force that the
cumbrous body was borne up several feet from the
ground ; but with its claws deeply fixed, the heavy
otter brought the eagle back to the earth. Grasshopper possessed himself of a handful of the prime
feathers, crowned his head with the trophy, and set
off in high spirits on the look out for something new.

After walking awhile, he came to a body of water
which flooded the trees on its banks—it was a
lake made by beavers. Taking his station on the
raised dam where the stream escaped, he watched to

see whether any of the beavers would show themselves. A head presently peeped out of the water to see who it was that disturbed them.

"My friend," said Grasshopper, in his most persuasive manner, "could you not oblige me by turning me into a beaver like yourself. Nothing would please me so much as to make your acquaintance, I can assure you;" for Grasshopper was curious to know how these watery creatures lived, and what kind of notions they had.

"I do not know," replied the beaver, who was rather short-nosed and surly. "I will go and ask the others. Meanwhile stay where you are, if you please."

"To be sure," answered Grasshopper, stealing down the bank several paces as soon as the beaver's back was turned.

Presently there was a great splashing of the water, and all the beavers showed their heads, and looked warily to where he stood, to see if he was armed; but he had knowingly left his bow and arrows in a hollow tree at a short distance.

After a long conversation, which they conducted in a whisper so that Grasshopper could not catch a word, strain his ears as he would, they all advanced in a body toward the spot where he stood; the chief approaching the nearest, and lifting his head highest out of the water.

"Can you not," said Grasshopper, noticing that they waited for him to speak first, "turn me into a beaver? I wish to live among you."

"Yes," answered their chief; "lie down." And Grasshopper in a moment found himself a beaver, and was gliding into the water, when a thought seemed to strike him, and he paused at the edge of the lake. "I am very small," he said, to the beaver, in a sorrowful tone. "You must make me large," he said; for Grasshopper was terribly ambitious, and wanted always to be the first person in every company. "Larger than any of you; in my present size it's hardly worth my while to go into the water."

"Yes, yes!" said they. "By and by, when we get into the lodge it shall be done."

They all dived into the lake, and in passing great heaps of limbs and logs at the bottom, he asked the use of them; they answered, "It is for our winter's provisions."

When they all got into the lodge their number was about one hundred. The lodge was large and warm.

"Now we will make you large," said they. "Will *that* do?"

"Yes," he answered; for he found that he was ten times the size of the largest.

"You need not go out," said the others; "we

will bring you food into the lodge, and you will be our chief."

" Very well," Grasshopper answered. He thought, "I will stay here and grow fat at their expense." But, soon after, one ran into the lodge, out of breath, crying out, " We are visited by the Indians !"

All huddled together in great fear. The water began to lower, for the hunters had broken down the dam, and they soon heard them on the roof of the lodge, breaking it up. Out jumped all the beavers into the water, and so escaped.

Grasshopper tried to follow them ; but, unfortunately, to gratify his ambition, they had made him so large that he could not creep out at the hole. He tried to call them back, but either they did not hear or would not attend to him ; he worried himself so much in searching for a door to let him out, that he looked like a great bladder, swollen and blistering in the sun, and the sweat stood out upon his forehead in knobs aud huge bubbles.

Although he heard and understood every word that the hunters spoke—and some of their expressions suggested terrible ideas—he could not turn himself back into a man. He had chosen to be a beaver, and a beaver he must be. One of the hunters, a prying little man, with a single lock dangling over one eye— this inquisitive little fellow put his head in at the top of the lodge. " *Ty-au !*" cried he. " *Tut ty-au!*

Me-shau-mik—king of beavers is in." Whereupon
the whole crowd of hunters began upon him with
their clubs, and knocked his scull about until it was
no harder than a morass in the middle of summer.
Grasshopper thought as well as ever he did, although
he was a beaver ; and he felt that he was in a rather
foolish scrape, inhabiting the carcass of a beaver.

Presently seven or eight of the hunters hoisted his
body upon long poles, and marched away home with
him. As they went, he reflected in this manner :
" What will become of me ? My ghost or shadow
will not die after they get me to their lodges."

Invitations were immediately sent out for a grand
feast ; but as soon as his body got cold, his soul
being uncomfortable in a house without heat, flew
off.

Having reassumed his mortal shape, Grasshopper
found himself standing near a prairie. After walking a distance, he saw a herd of elk feeding. He
admired their apparent ease and enjoyment of life,
and thought there could be nothing more pleasant than the liberty of running about and feeding on
the prairies. He had been a water animal and now he
wished to become a land animal, to learn what passed
in an elk's head as he roved about. He asked them
if they could not turn him into one of themselves.

" Yes," they answered, after a pause. " Get down
on your hands and feet."

He obeyed their directions, and forthwith **found** himself to be an elk.

"I want big horns, big feet," said he; "I wish to be very large;" for all the conceit and vain-glory had not been knocked out of Grasshopper, even by the sturdy thwacks of the hunters' clubs.

"Yes, yes," they answered. "There," exerting their power, "are you big enough?"

"That will do," he replied; for, looking into a take hard by, Grasshopper saw that he was very large. They spent their time in grazing and running to and fro; but what astonished Grasshopper, although he often lifted up his head and directed his eyes that way, he could never see the stars, which he had so admired as a human being.

Being rather cold, one day, Grasshopper went into a thick wood for shelter, whither he was followed by most of the herd. They had not been long there when some elks from behind passed the others like a strong wind, calling out:

"The hunters are after us!"

All took the alarm, and off they ran, Grasshopper with the rest.

"Keep out on the plains," they said. But it was too late to profit by this advice, for they had already got entangled in the thick woods. Grasshopper soon scented the hunters, who were closely following his trail, for they had left all the others and were making after him in full cry. He jumped furiously, dashed through the underwood, and broke down whole groves of saplings in his flight. But this only made it the harder for him to get on, such a huge and lusty elk was he by his own request.

Presently, as he dashed past an open space, he felt an arrow in his side. They could not well miss it, he presented so wide a mark to the shot. He bounded over trees under the smart, but the shafts clattered thicker and thicker at his ribs, and at last one entered his heart. He fell to the ground, and heard the whoop of triumph sounded by the hunters. On coming up, they looked on the carcass with astonishment, and with their hands up to their mouths, exclaimed: " *Ty-au! ty-au!*"

There were about sixty in the party, who had come out on a special hunt, as one of their number had, the day before, observed his large tracks on the plains. When they had skinned him his flesh grew cold, and his spirit took its flight from the dead body, and Grasshopper found himself in human shape, with a bow and arrows.

But his passion for adventure was not yet cooled; for on coming to a large lake with a sandy beach, he saw a large flock of brant, and speaking to them in the brant language, he requested them to make a brant of him.

3

"Yes," they replied, at once; for the brant is a bird of a very obliging disposition.

"But I want to be very large," he said. There was no end to the ambition of little Grasshopper.

"Very well," they answered; and he soon found himself a large brant, all the others standing gazing in astonishment at his great size.

"You must fly as leader," they said.

"No," answered Grasshopper; "I will fly behind."

"Very well," rejoined the brant; "one thing more we have to say to you, brother Grasshopper" (for he had told them his name). "You must be careful, in flying, not to look down, for something may happen to you."

"Well, it is so," said he; and soon the flock rose up into the air, for they were bound north. They flew very fast—he behind. One day, while going with a strong wind, and as swift as their wings could flap, as they passed over a large village the Indians raised a great shout on seeing them, particularly on Grasshopper's account, for his wings were broader than two large mats. The village people made such a frightful noise that he forgot what had been told him about looking down. They were now scudding along as swift as arrows; and as soon as he brought his neck in and stretched it down to look at the shouters, his huge tail was caught by the wind, and over and over he was blown. He tried to right himself, but without success, for he had no sooner got out of one heavy air-current than he fell into another, which treated him even more rudely than that he had escaped from. Down, down he went, making more turns than he wished for, from a height of several miles.

The first moment he had to look about him, Grasshopper, in the shape of a big brant, was aware that he was jammed into a large hollow tree. To get backward or forward was out of the question, and there, in spite of himself, was Grasshopper forced to tarry till his brant life was ended by starvation, when, his spirit being at liberty, he was once more a human being.

As he journeyed on in search of further adventures, Grasshopper came to a lodge in which were two old men, with heads white from extreme age. They were very fine old men to look at. There was such sweetness and innocence in their features that Grasshopper would have enjoyed himself very much at their lodge, if he had had no other entertainment than such as the gazing upon the serene and happy faces of the two innocent old men with heads white from extreme age afforded.

They treated him well, and he made known to them that he was going back to his village, his friends and people, whereupon the two white-headed old men very heartily wished him a good journey and abundance of comfort in seeing his friends once more. They even arose, old and infirm as they were, and tottering with exceeding difficulty to the door, were at great pains to point out to him the exact course he should take; and they called his attention to the circumstance that it was much shorter and more direct than he would have taken himself. Ah! what merry deceivers were these two old men with very white heads.

Grasshopper, with blessings showered on him until he was fairly out of sight, set forth with good heart. He thought he heard loud laughter resounding after him in the direction of the lodge of the two old men; but it could not have been the two old men, for they were, certainly, too old to laugh.

He walked briskly all day, and at night he had the satisfaction of reaching a lodge in all respects like that which he had left in the morning. There were two fine old men, and his treatment was in every particular the same, even down to the parting blessing and the laughter that followed him as he went his way.

After walking the third day, and coming to a lodge the same as before, he was satisfied from the bearings of the course he had taken that he had been journeying in a circle, and by a notch which he had cut in the door-post that these were the same two old men, all along; and that, despite their innocent

faces and their very white heads, they had been playing him a sorry trick.

"Who are you," said Grasshopper, " to treat me
so? Come forth, I say."

They were compelled to obey his summons, lest,
in his anger, he should take their lives; and they
appeared on the outside of the lodge.

"We must have a little trial of speed, now," said
Grasshopper.

"A race?" they asked. "We are very old; we
can not run."

"We will see," said Grasshopper; whereupon he
set them out upon the road, and then he gave them
a gentle push, which put them in motion. Then he
pushed them again—harder—harder—until they got
under fine head-way, when he gave each of them an
astounding shock with his foot, and off they flew at
a great rate, round and round the course; and such
was the magic virtue of the foot of Grasshopper,
that no object once set agoing by it could by any pos--
sibility stop; so that, for aught we know to the contrary, the two innocent, white-headed, merry old
men, are trotting with all their might and main
around the circle in which they beguiled Grasshopper, to this day.

Continuing his journey, Grasshopper, although
his head was warm and buzzing with all sorts of
schemes, did not know exactly what to do until he

came to a big lake. He mounted a high hill to try
and see to the other side, but he could not. He then
made a canoe, and sailed forth. The water was very
clear—a transparent blue—and he saw that it
abounded with fish of a rare and delicate complexion. This circumstance inspired him with a wish
to return to his village, and to bring his people to
live near this beautiful lake.

Toward evening, coming to a woody island, he encamped and ate the fish he had speared, and they
proved to be as comforting to the stomach as they
were pleasing to the eye. The next day Grasshopper returned to the main land, and as he wandered
along the shore he espied at a distance the celebrated giant, Manabozho, who is a bitter enemy of
Grasshopper, and loses no opportunity to stop him
on his journeyings and to thwart his plans.

At first it occurred to Grasshopper to have a trial
of wits with the giant, but, on second thoughts, he
said to himself, "I am in a hurry now; I will see
him another time."

With no further mischief than raising a great
whirlwind of dust, which caused Manabozho to rub
his eyes severely, Grasshopper quietly slipped out of
the way ; and he made good speed withal, for in much
less time than you could count half the stars in the
sky of a winter night, he had reached home.

His return was welcomed with a great hubbub of

feasting and songs ; and he had scarcely set foot in the village before he had invitations to take pot-luck at different lodges, which would have lasted him the rest of his natural life. Pipe-bearer, who had some time before given up the cares of a ruler, and fallen back upon his native place, fairly danced with joy at the sight of Grasshopper, who, not to be outdone, dandled him affectionately in his arms, by casting him up and down in the air half a mile or so, till little Pipe-bearer had no breath left in his body to say that he was happy to see Grasshopper home again.

Grasshopper gave the village folks a lively account of his adventures, and when he came to the blue lake and the abundant fish, he dwelt upon their charms with such effect that they agreed, with one voice, that it must be a glorious place to live in, and if he would show them the way they would shift camp and settle there at once.

He not only showed them the way, but bringing his wonderful strength and speed of foot to bear, in less than half a day he had transported the whole village, with its children, women, tents, and implements of war, to the new water-side.

Here, for a time, Grasshopper appeared to be content, until one day a message came for him in the shape of a bear, who said that their king wished to see him immediately at his village. Grasshopper was ready in an instant ; and mounting upon the

messenger's back, off he ran. Toward evening they
climbed a high mountain, and came to a cave where
the bear-king lived. He was a very large person ;
and puffing with fat and a sense of his own importance, he made Grasshopper welcome by inviting him
in to his lodge.

As soon as it was proper, he spoke, and said that
he had sent for him on hearing that he was the chief
who was moving a large party toward his hunting-
grounds.

" You must know," said the bear-king with a terrible growl, "that you have no right there, and I
wish you would leave the country with your party,
or else the strongest force will take possession. Take
notice."

" Very well," replied Grasshopper, going toward
the door, for he suspected that the king of the bears
was preparing to give him a hug. " So be it."

He wished to gain time, and to consult his people ;
for he had seen as he came along that the bears were
gathering in great force on the side of the mountain.
He also made known to the bear-king that he would
go back that night that his people might be put in
immediate possession of his royal behest.

The bear-king replied that Grasshopper might do
as he pleased, but that one of his young men was at
his command ; and, jumping nimbly on his back,
Grasshopper rode home.

He assembled the people, and ordered the bear's head off, to be hung outside of the village, that the bear-spies, who were lurking in the neighborhood, might see it and carry the news to their chief.

The next morning, by break of day, Grasshopper had all of his young warriors under arms and ready for a fight. About the middle of the afternoon the bear war-party came in sight, led on by the pursy king, and making a tremendous noise. They advanced on their hind-legs, and made a very imposing display of their teeth and eyeballs.

The bear-chief himself came forward, and with a majestic waive of his right hand, said that he did not wish to shed the blood of the young warriors ; but that if Grasshopper, who appeared to be the head of the war-party, consented, they two would have a race, and the winner should kill the losing chief, and all his young men should be servants to the other.

Grasshopper agreed, of course—how little Pipe-bearer, who stood by, grinned as they came to terms !—and they started to run before the whole company of warriors who stood in a circle looking on.

At first there was a prospect that Grasshopper would be badly beaten ; for although he kept crowding the great fat bear-king till the sweat trickled from his shaggy ears, he never seemed to be able to push past him. By and by, Grasshopper, going through a number of the most extraordinary maneuvers in

the world, raised about the great fat bear-king such
eddies and whirlwinds with the sand, and so danced
about, before and after him, that he at last got fairly
bewildered, and cried out for them to come and take
him off. Out of sight before him in reaching the
goal, Grasshopper only waited for the bear-king to
come up, when he drove an arrow straight through
him, and ordered them to take the body away and
make it ready for supper; as he was getting hungry.

He then directed all of the other bears to fall to
and help prepare the feast; for in fulfillment of the
agreement they had become servants. With many
wry faces the bears, although bound to act becomingly
in their new character, according to the forfeit, served
up the body of their late royal master; and in doing
this they fell, either by accident or design, into many
curious mistakes.

When the feast came to be served up, and they
were summoned to be in attendance, one of them, a
sprightly young fellow of an inquisitive turn of
mind, was found upon the roof of the lodge, with
his head half way down the smoke-hole, with a view
to learn what they were to have for dinner. Another,
a middle-aged bear with very long arms, who was
put in charge of the children in the character of
nurse, squeezed three or four of the most promising
young papooses to death, while the mothers were
outside to look after the preparations; and another,

THE BEAR SERVANTS. Page 59.

when he should have been waiting at the back of
his master, had climbed a shady tree and was in-
dulging in his afternoon nap. And when, at last,
the dinner was ready to be served, they came tumbling in with the dishes, heels over head, one after
the other, so that one half of the feast was spread
upon the ground, and the other half deposited out
of doors, on the other side of the lodge.

After a while, however, by strict discipline, and
threatening to cut off their provisions, the bear-serv-
ants were brought into tolerable control.

Yet Grasshopper, with his ever restless disposition,
was uneasy; and, having done so many wonderful
things, he resolved upon a strict and thorough re-
form in all the affairs of the village. To prevent future difficulty, he determined to adopt new regula-
tions between the bears and their masters.

With this view, he issued an edict that hencefor-
ward the bears should eat at the first table, and that
the Indians were to wait upon them; that in all public processions of an honorable character the bears
should go first; and that when any fighting was to
be done, the Indians should have the privilege reserved of receiving the first shots. A special exemp-
tion was made in behalf of Grasshopper's favorite and
confidential adviser, the Pipe-bearer (who had been
very busy in private, recommending the new order of
things), who was to be allowed to sit at the head of

the feast, and to stay at home with the old women in the event of battle.

Having seen his orders strictly enforced, and the rights of the bears over the Indians fairly established, Grasshopper fixed his mind upon further adventures. He determined to go abroad for a time, and having an old score to settle with Manabozho, he set out with a hope of soon falling in with that famous giant. Grasshopper was a blood relation of Dais Imid, or He of the Little Shell, and had heard of what had passed between that giant and his kinsman.

After wandering a long time he came to the lodge of Manabozho, who was absent. He thought he must play him a trick; and so he turned every thing in the lodge upside down, and killed his birds, of which there was an extraordinary attendance, for Manabozho is master of the fowls of the air, and this was the appointed morning for them to call and pay their court to him. Among the number was a raven, accounted the meanest of birds, which Grasshopper killed and hung up by the neck, to insult him.

He then went on till he came to a very high point of rocks running out into the lake, from the top of which he could see the country, back as far as the eye could reach. While sitting there, Manabozho's mountain chickens flew around and past him in great numbers. Out of mere spite to their master, Grasshopper shot them by the score, for his arrows were very sure and the birds very plenty, and he amused himself by throwing the birds down the rocks. At length a wary bird cried out:

"Grasshopper is killing us; go and tell our father."

Away sped a delegation of the birds which were the quickest of wing, and Manabozho soon made his appearance on the plain below. Grasshopper, who, when he is in the wrong, is no match for Manabozho, made his escape on the other side. Manabozho, who had in two or three strides reached the top of the mountain, cried out:

"You are a rogue. The earth is not so large but I can get up to you."

Off ran Grasshopper and Manabozho after him. The race was sharp; and such leaps and strides as they made! Over hills and prairies, with all his speed, went Grasshopper, and Manabozho hard upon him. Grasshopper had some mischievous notions still left in his head which he thought might befriend him. He knew that Manabozho was under a spell to restore whatever he, Grasshopper, destroyed. Forthwith he stopped and climbed a large pine-tree, stripped off its beautiful green foliage, threw it to the winds, and then went on.

When Manabozho reached the spot, the tree addressed him: "Great chief," said the tree, "will you give my life again? Grasshopper has killed me."

"Yes," replied Manabozho, who, as quickly as he could, gathered the scattered leaves and branches, renewed its beauty with his breath, and set off. Although Grasshopper in the same way compelled Manabozho to lose time in repairing the hemlock, the sycamore, cedar, and many other trees, the giant did not falter, but pushing briskly forward, was fast overtaking him, when Grasshopper happened to see an elk. And asking him, for old acquaintance' sake, to take him on his back, the elk did so, and for some time he made good headway, but still Manabozho was in sight.

He was fast gaining upon him, when Grasshopper threw himself off the elk's back; and striking a great sandstone rock near the path, he broke it into pieces, and scattered the grains in a thousand directions; for this was nearly his last hope of escape. Manabozho was so close upon him at this place that he had almost caught him; but the foundation of the rock cried out,

"Haye! Ne-me-sho, Grasshopper has spoiled me. Will you not restore me to life?"

"Yes," replied Manabozho. He re-established the rock in all its strength.

He then pushed on in pursuit, and had got so near to Grasshopper as to put out his arm to seize him; but Grasshopper dodged him, and, as his last chance, he immediately raised such a dust and commotion by whirlwinds, as made the trees break and the sand and leaves dance in the air. Again and again Manabozho stretched his arm, but he escaped him at every turn, and kept up such a tumult of dust that he dashed into a hollow tree which had been blown down, changed himself into a snake, and crept out at the roots just in time to save his life; for at that moment Manabozho, who had the power of lightning, struck it, and it was strewn about in little pieces.

Again Grasshopper was in human shape, and Manabozho was pressing him hard. At a distance he saw a very high bluff of rocks jutting out into a lake, and he ran for the foot of the precipice which was abrupt and elevated. As he came near, to his surprise and great relief, the Manito of the rock opened his door and told Grasshopper to come in. The door was no sooner closed than Manabozho knocked.

"Open it!" he cried, with a loud voice. The Manito was afraid of him; but he said to Grasshopper, "Since I have taken you as my guest, I would sooner die with you than open the door."

"Open it!" Manabozho again cried, in a louder voice than before.

The Manito kept silent. Manabozho, however, made no attempt to open it by force. He waited a few moments.

"Very well," he said; "I give you till morning to live."

Grasshopper trembled, for he thought his last hour had come; but the Manito bade him to be of good cheer.

When the night came on the clouds were thick and black, and as they were torn open by the lightning, such discharges of thunder were never heard as bellowed forth. The clouds advanced slowly and wrapped the earth about with their vast shadows as in a huge cloak. All night long the clouds gathered, and the lightning flashed, and the thunder roared, and above all could be heard Manabozho muttering vengeance upon poor little Grasshopper.

"You have led a very foolish kind of life, Grasshopper," said his friend the Manito.

"I know it—I know it!" Grasshopper answered.

"You had great gifts of strength awarded to you," said the Manito.

"I am aware of it," replied Grasshopper.

"Instead of employing it for useful purposes, and for the good of your fellow-creatures, you have done nothing since you became a man but raise whirlwinds on the highways, leap over trees, break whatever you met in pieces, and perform a thousand idle pranks."

Grasshopper, with great penitence, confessed that his friend the Manito spoke but too truly; and at last his entertainer, with a still more serious manner, said :

"Grasshopper, you still have your gift of strength. Dedicate it to the good of mankind. Lay all of these wanton and vain-glorious notions out of your head. In a word, be as good as you are strong."

"I will," answered Grasshopper. "My heart is changed; I see the error of my ways."

Black and stormy as it had been all night, when morning came the sun was shining, the air was soft and sweet as the summer down and the blown rose; and afar off upon the side of a mountain sat Manabozho, his head upon his knees, languid and cast down in spirit. His power was gone, for now Grasshopper was in the right, and he could touch him no more.

With many thanks, Grasshopper left the good Manito, taking the nearest way home to his own people.

As he passed on, he fell in with an old man who was wandering about the country in search of some place which he could not find. As soon as he learned his difficulty, Grasshopper, placing the old man upon his back, hurried away, and in a short hour's dispatch of foot set him down among his own kindred, of whom he had been in quest.

Loosing no time, Grasshopper next came to an open plain, where a small number of men stood at bay, and on the very point of being borne down by great odds, in a force of armed warriors, fierce of aspect and of prodigious strength. When Grasshopper saw this unequal struggle, rushing forward he seized a long bare pole, and, wielding it with his whole force, he drove the fierce warriors back; and, laying about him on every hand, he soon sent them a thousand ways in great haste, and in a very sore plight.

Without tarrying to receive the thanks of those to whom he had brought this timely relief, he made his utmost speed, and by the close of the afternoon he had come in sight of his own village. What were his surprise and horror, as he approached nearer, to discover the bears in excellent case and flesh, seated at lazy leisure in the trees, looking idly on while his brother Indians, for their pastime, were dancing a fantastic and wearisome dance, in the course of which they were frequently compelled to go upon all fours and bow their heads in profound obeisance to their bear-masters in the trees.

As he drew nearer, his heart sunk within him to see how starved, and hollow-eyed, and woe-begone they were; and his horror was at its height when, as he entered his own lodge, he beheld his favorite and friend, the Pipe-bearer, also on all fours, smoothing the floor with the palms of his hands to make it a comfortable sitting-place for the bears on their return from the dance.

It did not take Grasshopper a long time to resolve what he should do. He immediately resumed power in the village, bestowed a sound cudgeling upon the bears, and sent them off to live in the mountains, among their own people, as bears should; restored to the people all their rights; gave them plenty to eat and drink; exerting his great strength in hunting, in rebuilding their lodges, keeping in check their enemies, and doing all the good he could to every body.

Peace and plenty soon shone and showered upon the spot; and, never once thinking of all his wild and wanton frolics, the people blessed Grasshopper for all his kindness, and sincerely prayed that his name might be held in honor for a thousand years to come, as no doubt it will.

Little Pipe-bearer stood by Grasshopper in all his course, and admired his ways as much now that he had taken to being orderly and useful, as in the old times, when he was walking a mile a minute, and in mere wantonness bringing home whole forests in his arms for fire-wood, in midsummer.

It was a great old age to which Grasshopper lived, and when at last he came to die, there was not a dry eye in all that part of the world where he spent his latter days.

V.

THE TWO JEEBI.

THERE lived a hunter in the North, who had a wife and one child. His lodge stood far off in the forest, several days' journey from any other. He spent his days in hunting, and his evenings in relating to his wife the incidents that had befallen him. As game was very abundant, he found no difficulty in killing as much as they wanted. Just in all his acts, he lived a peaceful and happy life.

One evening during the winter season, it chanced that he remained out longer than usual, and his wife began to fear that some accident had befallen him. It was already dark. She listened attentively, and at last heard the sound of approaching footsteps.

Not doubting that it was her husband, she went to the door and beheld two strange females. She bade them enter, and invited them to remain. She observed that they were total strangers in the country. There was something so peculiar in their looks, air and manner, that she was disturbed by their presence. They would not come near to the fire. They sat in a remote part of the lodge, shy and taciturn, and drew their garments about them in such a manner as nearly to hide their faces. So far as she could judge, they were pale, hollow-eyed, and long-visaged, very thin and emaciated.

There was but little light in the lodge, as the fire was low, and its fitful flashes, by disclosing their white faces and then dropping them in sudden darkness, served rather to increase than to dispel her fears.

"Merciful Spirit!" cried a voice from the opposite part of the lodge; "there are two corpses clothed with garments!"

The hunter's wife turned around, but seeing nobody save her little child, staring across from under his blanket, she said to herself, "The boy can not speak; the sounds were but the gusts of wind." She trembled, and was ready to sink to the earth.

Her husband at this moment entered, and in some measure relieved her alarm. He threw down the carcass of a large fat deer.

"Behold what a fine and fat animal!" cried the mysterious females; and they immediately ran and pulled off pieces of the whitest fat, which they greedily devoured.

The hunter and his wife looked on with astonishment, but remained silent. They supposed that their guests might have been stricken with famine.

The next day, however, the same unusual conduct was repeated. The strange females again tore off the fat and devoured it with eagerness. The third day, the hunter thought that he would anticipate their wants by tying up a share of the hunt, and placing it apart for their express use. They accepted it, but still appeared dissatisfied, and went to the wife's portion and tore off more.

The hunter and his wife were surprised at such rude and unaccountable conduct, but they remained silent, for they respected their guests, and had observed that they had been attended with marked good luck during the sojourn of these mysterious visitors in their lodge.

In other respects, the deportment of the females was strictly unexceptionable. They were modest, distant, and silent. They never uttered a word during the day. At night they would occupy themselves in procuring wood, which they carried to the lodge, and then, restoring the implements exactly where they had found them, resume their places without speaking. They were never known to stay out until daylight. They never laughed or jested.

The winter was nearly passed away, when, one evening, the hunter was abroad later than usual. The moment he came in and laid down his day's hunt, as was his custom, before his wife, the two females seized upon the deer and began to tear off the fat in so unceremonious a way that her anger was excited. She constrained herself, however, in a good degree, but she could not conceal her feelings, though she said but little.

The strange guests observed the state of her mind, and they became uneasy, and withdrew further still into the remote gloom of the lodge. The good hunter saw the eclipse that was darkening the quiet of his lodge, and carefully inquired of its cause; but his wife denied having used any words of complaining or reproach.

They retired to their couches, and the hunter tried to compose himself to sleep, but could not, for the sighs and sobs of the two females were incessant. He arose on his couch and addressed them as follows:

"Tell me," said he, "what is it that gives you pain of mind and causes you to bemoan your presence here. Has my wife given you offense, or trespassed upon the rights of hospitality?"

They replied in the negative. "We have been treated by you with kindness and affection. It is not for any slight we have received that we weep. Our mission is not to you only. We come from the other land to test mankind, and to try the sincerity of the living. Often we have heard the bereaved by death say that if the lost could be restored, they would devote their lives to make them happy. We have been moved by the bitter lamentations which have reached the place of the departed, and have come to make proof of the sincerity of those who have lost friends. We are your two dead sisters. Three moons were allotted us by the Master of Life to make the trial. More than half the time had been successfully passed, when the angry feelings of your wife indicated the irksomeness you felt at our presence, and has made us resolve on our departure."

They continued to talk to the hunter and his wife, gave them instructions as to a future life, and pronounced a blessing upon them.

"There is one point," they added, "of which we wish to speak. You have thought our conduct very strange and rude in possessing ourselves of the choicest parts of your hunt. *That* was the point of trial selected to put you to. It is the wife's peculiar privilege. You love your wife. For another to usurp what belongs to her, we know to be the severest test of her goodness of heart, and consequently of your temper and feelings. We knew your manners and customs, but we came to prove you, not by complying with but by violating them. Pardon us. We are the agents of him who sent us. Peace to your dwelling. Farewell !"

When they ceased, total darkness filled the lodge. No object could be seen. The inmates heard the lodge-door open and shut, but they never saw more of the Two Spirits.

The hunter found the success which they had promised. He became celebrated in the chase, and never wanted for any thing. He had many children, all of whom grew up to manhood ; and he who had lain in the lodge, a little child, while the Jeebi dwelt there, led them in all good deeds, and health, peace, and long life were the rewards of the hunter's hospitality.

4

VI.

OSSEO, THE SON OF THE EVENING STAR.

THERE once lived an Indian in the north who had ten daughters, all of whom grew up to womanhood. They were noted for their beauty, especially Oweenee, the youngest, who was very independent in her way of thinking. She was a great admirer of romantic places, and spent much of her time with the flowers and winds and clouds in the open air. Though the flower were homely, if it was fragrant— though the wind were rough, if it was healthful—and though the cloud were dark, if it embosomed the fruitful rain, she knew how, in spite of appearances, to acknowledge the good qualities concealed from the eye. She paid very little attention to the many handsome young men who came to her father's lodge for the purpose of seeing her.

Her elder sisters were all sought in marriage, and one after the other they went off to dwell in the lodges of their husbands; but Oweenee was deaf to all proposals of the kind. At last she married an old man called Osseo, who was scarcely able to walk, and who was too poor to have things like others. The only property he owned in the world was the walking-staff which he carried in his hand. Though thus poor and homely, Osseo was a devout and good man ; faithful in all his duties, and obedient in all things to the Good Spirit. Of course they jeered and laughed at Oweenee on all sides, but she seemed to be quite happy, and said to them, "It is my choice and you will see in the end who has acted the wisest."

They made a special mock of the walking-staff, and scarcely an hour in the day passed that they had not some disparaging reference to it. Among themselves they spoke of Osseo of the walking-staff, in derision, as the owner of the big woods, or the great timber-man.

"True " said Oweenee, "it is but a simple stick ; but as it supports the steps of my husband, it is more precious to me than all the forests of the north."

A time came when the sisters, and their husbands, and their parents were all invited to a feast. As the distance was considerable, they doubted whether Osseo, so aged and feeble, would be able to under-take the journey ; but in spite of their friendly doubts, he joined them, and set out with a good heart.

As they walked along the path they could not

help pitying their young and handsome sister who had such an unsuitable mate. She, however, smiled upon Osseo, and kept with him by the way the same as if he had been the comeliest bridegroom in all the company. Osseo often stopped and gazed upward ; but they could perceive nothing in the direction in which he looked, unless it was the faint glimmering of the evening star. They heard him muttering to himself as they went along, and one of the elder sisters caught the words, " Pity me, my father !"

" Poor old man," said she ; " he is talking to his father. What a pity it is that he would not fall and break his neck, that our sister might have a young husband."

Presently as they came to a great rock where Osseo had been used to breathe his morning and his evening prayer, the star emitted a brighter ray, which shone directly in his face. Osseo, with a sharp cry, fell trembling to the earth, where the others would have left him, but his good wife raised him up, and he sprang forward on the path, and with steps light as the reindeer he led the party, no longer decrepid and infirm, but a beautiful young man. On turning around to look for his wife, behold she had become changed, at the same moment, into an aged and feeble woman, bent almost double, and walking with the staff which he had cast aside.

Osseo immediately joined her, and with looks of fondness and the tenderest regard, bestowed on her every endearing attention, and constantly addressed her by the term of ne-ne-moosh-a, or my sweetheart.

As they walked along, whenever they were not gazing fondly in each other's face, they bent their looks on heaven, and a light, as if of far-off stars, was in their eyes.

On arriving at the lodge of the hunter with whom they were to feast, they found the banquet ready, and as soon as their entertainer had finished his harangue—in which he told them his feasting was in honor of the Evening or Woman's Star—they began to partake of the portion dealt out, according to age and character, to each one of the guests. The food was very delicious, and they were all happy but Osseo, who looked at his wife, and then gazed upward, as if he was looking into the substance of the sky. Sounds were soon heard, as if from far-off voices in the air, and they became plainer and plainer, till he could clearly distinguish some of the words.

"My son, my son," said the voice; "I have seen your afflictions, and pity your wants. I come to call you away from a scene that is stained with blood and tears. The earth is full of sorrows. Wicked spirits, the enemies of mankind, walk abroad, and lie in wait to ensnare the children of the sky. Every night they

are lifting their voices to the Power of Evil, and every
day they make themselves busy in casting mischief in
the hunter's path. You have long been their victim,
but you shall be their victim no more. The spell you
were under is broken. Your evil genius is overcome.
I have cast him down by my superior strength, and it
is this strength I now exert for your happiness. Ascend, my son; ascend into the skies, and partake of
the feast I have prepared for you in the stars, and
bring with you those you love.

" The food set before you is enchanted and blessed.
Fear not to partake of it. It is endowed with magic
power to give immortality to mortals, and to change
men to spirits. Your bowls and kettles shall no
longer be wood and earth. The one shall become silver, and the other pure gold. They shall shine like fire,
and glisten like the most beautiful scarlet. Every female shall also change her state and looks, and no
longer be doomed to laborious tasks. She shall put
on the beauty of the star-light, and become a shining
bird of the air. She shall dance, and not work. She
shall sing, and not cry.

" My beams," continued the voice, " shine faintly
on your lodge, but they have power to transform it
into the lightness of the skies, and decorate it with
the colors of the clouds. Come, Osseo, my son, and
dwell no longer on earth. Think strongly on my
words, and look steadfastly at my beams. My power

is now at its height. Doubt not, delay not. It is the voice of the Spirit of the Stars that calls you away to happiness and celestial rest."

The words were intelligible to Osseo, but his companions thought them some far-off sounds of music, or birds singing in the woods. Very soon the lodge began to shake and tremble, and they felt it rising into the air. It was too late to run out, for they were already as high as the tops of the trees. Osseo looked around him as the lodge passed through the topmost boughs, and behold! their wooden dishes were changed into shells of a scarlet color, the poles of the lodge to glittering rods of silver, and the bark that covered them into the gorgeous wings of insects.

A moment more and his brothers and sisters, and their parents and friends, were transformed into birds of various plumage. Some were jays, some partridges and pigeons, and others gay singing birds, who hopped about, displaying their many-colored feathers, and singing songs of cheerful note.

But his wife, Oweenee, still kept her earthly garb, and exhibited all the indications of extreme old age. He again cast his eyes in the direction of the clouds, and uttered the peculiar cry which had given him the victory at the rock. In a moment the youth and beauty of his wife returned; her dingy garments assumed the shining appearance of green silk, and her staff was changed into a silver feather

The lodge again shook and trembled, for they were now passing through the uppermost clouds, and they immediately after found themselves in the Evening Star, the residence of Osseo's father.

"My son," said the old man, "hang that cage of birds which you have brought along in your hand at the door, and I will inform you why you and your wife have been sent for."

Osseo obeyed, and then took his seat in the lodge.

"Pity was shown to you," resumed the King of the Star, "on account of the contempt of your wife's sister, who laughed at her ill fortune, and ridiculed you while you were under the power of that wicked spirit whom you overcame at the rock. That spirit lives in the next lodge, being the small star you see on the left of mine, and he has always felt envious of my family because we had greater power, and especially that we had committed to us the care of the female world. He failed in many attempts to destroy your brothers and sisters-in-law, but succeeded at last in transforming yourself and your wife into decrepid old persons. You must be careful and not let the light of his beams fall on you, while you are here, for therein lies the power of his enchantment. A ray of light is the bow and arrow he uses."

Osseo lived happy and contented in the parental lodge, and in due time his wife presented him with a son, who grew up rapidly, and in the very likeness of Osseo himself. He was very quick and ready in learning every thing that was done in his grandfather's dominions, but he wished also to learn the art of hunting, for he had heard that this was a favorite pursuit below. To gratify him, his father made him a bow and arrows, and he then let the birds out of the cage that he might practice in shooting. In this pastime he soon became expert, and the very first day he brought down a bird; but when he went to pick it up, to his amazement it was a beautiful young woman, with the arrow sticking in her breast. It was one of his younger aunts.

The moment her blood fell upon the surface of that pure and spotless planet, the charm was dissolved. The boy immediately found himself sinking, although he was partly upheld by something like wings until he passed through the lower clouds, and he then suddenly dropped upon a high, breezy island in a large lake. He was pleased, on looking up, to see all his aunts and uncles following him in the form of birds, and he soon discovered the silver lodge, with his father and mother, descending, with its waving tassels fluttering like so many insects' gilded wings. It rested on the loftiest cliffs of the island, and there they fixed their residence. They all resumed their natural shapes, but they were diminished to the size of fairies; and as a mark of homage to the King of the Evening Star, they never failed on every pleasant evening during the summer season to join hands and dance upon the top of the rocks. These rocks were quickly observed by the Indians to be covered, in moonlight evenings, with a larger sort of Ininees, or little men, and were called Mish-in-e-mok-in-ok-ong, or Little Spirits, and the island is named from them to this day.

Their shining lodge can be seen in the summer evenings, when the moon beams strongly on the pinnacles of the rocks; and the fishermen who go near those high cliffs at night, have even heard the voices of the happy little dancers. And Osseo and his wife, as fondly attached to each other as ever, always lead the dance.

VII.

GRAY EAGLE AND HIS FIVE BROTHERS.

THERE were six falcons living in a nest, five of whom were still too young to fly, when it so happened that both the parent birds were shot in one day. The young brood waited anxiously for their return ; but night came, and they were left without parents and without food.

Gray Eagle, the eldest, and the only one whose feathers had become stout enough to enable him to leave the nest, took his place at the head of the family, and assumed the duty of stifling their cries and providing the little household with food, in which he was very successful. But, after a short time had passed, by an unlucky mischance, while out on a foraging excursion, he got one of his wings broken. This was the more to be regretted, as the season had arrived when they were soon to go to a southern country to pass the winter, and the children were only waiting to become a little stronger and more expert on the wing to set out on the journey.

Finding that their elder brother did not return, they resolved to go in search of him. After beating up and down the country for the better part of a whole day, they at last found him, sorely wounded and unable to fly, lodged in the upper branches of a sycamore-tree.

"Brothers," said Gray Eagle, as soon as they were gathered around, and questioned him as to the extent of his injuries, "an accident has befallen me, but let not this prevent your going to a warmer climate. Winter is rapidly approaching, and you can not remain here. It is better that I alone should die, than for you all to suffer on my account."

"No, no," they replied, with one voice. "We will not forsake you. We will share your sufferings; we will abandon our journey, and take care of you as you did of us before we were able to take care of ourselves. If the chill climate kills you, it shall kill us. Do you think we can so soon forget your brotherly care, which has equaled a father's, and even a mother's kindness? Whether you live or die, we will live or die with you."

They sought out a hollow tree to winter in, and contrived to carry their wounded nest-mate thither; and before the rigor of the season had set in, they had, by diligence and economy, stored up food enough to carry them through the winter months.

To make the provisions they had laid in last the

better, it was agreed among them that two of their
number should go south ; leaving the other three to
watch over, feed, and protect their wounded brother.
The travelers set forth, sorry to leave home, but
resolved that the first promise of spring should bring
them back again. At the close of day, the three
brothers who remained, mounting to the very peak
of the tree, and bearing Gray Eagle in their arms,
watched them, as they vanished away southward, till
their forms blended with the air and were wholly
lost to sight.

Their next business was to set the household in
order, and this, with the judicious direction of Gray
Eagle, who was propped up in a snug fork, with soft
cushions of dry moss, they speedily accomplished.
One of the sisters, for there were two of these, took
upon herself the charge of nursing Gray Eagle, preparing his food, bringing him water, and changing
his pillows when he grew tired of one position. She
also looked to it that the house itself was kept in a
tidy condition, and that the pantry was supplied
with food. The second brother was assigned the
duty of physician, and he was to prescribe such herbs
and other medicines as the state of the health of
Gray Eagle seemed to require. As the second brother had no other invalid on his visiting-list, he devoted the time not given to the cure of his patient,
to the killing of game wherewith to stock the house-

keeper's larder ; so that, whatever he did, he was always busy in the line of professional duty—killing or curing. On his hunting excursions, Doctor Falcon carried with him his youngest brother, who, being a foolish young fellow, and inexperienced in the ways of the world, it was not thought safe to trust alone.

In due time, what with good nursing, and good feeding, and good air, Gray Eagle recovered from his wound, and he repaid the kindness of his brothers by giving them such advice and instruction in the art of hunting as his age and experience qualified him to impart. As spring advanced, they began to look about for the means of replenishing their store-house, whose supplies were running low; and they were all quite successful in their quest except the youngest, whose name was Peepi, or the Pigeon-Hawk, and who had of late begun to set up for himself. Being small and foolish, and feather-headed, flying hither and yonder without any set purpose, it so happened that Peepi always came home, so to phrase it, with an empty game-bag, and his pinions terribly rumpled.

At last Gray Eagle spoke to him, and demanded the cause of his ill-luck.

"It is not my smallness nor weakness of body," Peepi answered, "that prevents my bringing home provender as well as my brothers. I am all the time on the wing, hither and thither. I kill ducks and other birds every time I go out; but just as I get to the woods, on my way home, I am met by a large ko-ko-ho, who robs me of my prey; and,' added Peepi, with great energy, "it's my settled opinion that the villain lies in wait for the very purpose of doing so."

"I have no doubt you are right, Brother Peepi," rejoined Gray Eagle. "I know this pirate—his name is White Owl; and now that I feel my strength fully recovered, I will go out with you to-morrow and help you look after this greedy bush-ranger."

The next day they went forth in company, and arrived at a fine fresh-water lake. Gray Eagle seated himself hard by, while Peepi started out, and soon pounced upon a duck.

"Well done!" thought his brother, who saw his success; but just as little Peepi was getting to land with his prize, up sailed a large white owl from a tree where he, too, had been watching, and laid claim to it. He was on the point of wresting it from Peepi, when Gray Eagle, calling out to the intruder to desist, rushed up, and, fixing his talons in both sides of the owl, without further introduction or ceremony, flew away with him.

The little Pigeon-Hawk followed closely, with the duck under his wing, rejoiced and happy to think that he had something to carry home at last. He was naturally much vexed with the owl, and had no sooner delivered over the duck to his sister, the housekeeper, than he flew in the owl s face, and, venting an abundance of reproachful terms, would, in his passion, have torn the very eyes out of the White Owl's head.

"Softly, Peepi," said the Gray Eagle, stepping in between them. "Don't be in such a huff, my little brother, nor exhibit so revengeful a temper. Do you not know that we are to forgive our enemies? White Owl, you may go; but let this be a lesson to you, not to play the tyrant over those who may chance to be weaker than yourself."

So, after adding to this much more good advice, and telling him what kind of herbs would cure his wounds, Gray Eagle dismissed White Owl, and the four brothers and sisters sat down to supper.

The next day, betimes, in the morning, before the household had fairly rubbed the cobwebs out of the corners of their eyes, there came a knock at the front door—which was a dry branch that lay down before the hollow of the tree in which they lodged—and being called to come in, who should make their appearance but the two nest-mates, who had just returned from the South, where they had been wintering. There was great rejoicing over their return, and now that they were all happily re-united, each one soon chose a mate and began to keep house in the woods for himself.

Spring had now revisited the North. The cold

winds had all blown themselves away, the ice had melted, the streams were open, and smiled as they looked at the blue sky once more; and the forests, far and wide, in their green mantle, echoed every cheerful sound.

But it is in vain that spring returns, and that the heart of Nature is opened in bounty, if we are not thankful to the Master of Life, who has preserved us through the winter. Nor does that man answer the end for which he was made who does not show a kind and charitable feeling to all who are in want or sickness, especially to his blood relations.

The love and harmony of Gray Eagle and his brothers continued. They never forgot each other. Every week, on the fourth afternoon of the week (for that was the time when they had found their wounded elder brother), they had a meeting in the hollow of the old sycamore-tree, when they talked over family matters, and advised with each other, as brothers should, about their affairs.

VIII.

THE TOAD-WOMAN.

GREAT good luck once happened to a young woman who was living all alone in the woods with
nobody near her but her little dog; for, to her surprise,
she found fresh meat every morning at her door. She
was very curious to know who it was that supplied
her, and watching one morning, just as the sun had
risen, she saw a handsome young man gliding away
into the forest. Having seen her, he became her
husband, and she had a son by him.

One day, not long after this, he did not return at
evening, as usual, from hunting. She waited till late
at night, but he came no more.

The next day, she swung her child to sleep in its
cradle, and then said to her dog, "Take care of your
brother while I am gone, and when he cries, halloo
for me."

The cradle was made of the finest wampum, and
all its bandages and ornaments were of the same
precious stuff.

After a short time, the woman heard the cry of the dog, and running home as fast as she could, she found her child gone, and the dog too. On looking around, she saw scattered upon the ground pieces of the wampum of her child's cradle, and she knew that the dog had been faithful, and had striven his best to save her child from being carried off, as he had been, by an old woman, from a distant country, called Mukakee Mindemoea, or the Toad-Woman.

The mother hurried off at full speed in pursuit, and as she flew along, she came, from time to time, to lodges inhabited by old women, who told her at what time the child-thief had passed; they also gave her shoes that she might follow on. There was a number of these old women who seemed as if they were prophetesses, and knew what was to come long beforehand. Each of them would say to her that when she had arrived at the next lodge, she must set the toes of the moccasins they had given her pointing homeward, and that they would return of themselves. The young woman was very careful to send back in this manner all the shoes she borrowed.

She thus followed in the pursuit, from valley to valley, and stream to stream, for many months and years; when she came at length to the lodge of the last of the friendly old grandmothers, as they were called, who gave her the last instructions how to proceed. She told her that she was near the place where her son was to be found; and she directed her to build a lodge of cedar-boughs, hard by the old Toad-Woman's lodge, and to make a little bark dish, and to fill it with the juice of the wild grape.

"Then," she said, "your first child (meaning the dog) will come and find you out."

These directions the young woman followed just as they had been given to her, and in a short time she heard her son, now grown up, going out to hunt, with his dog, calling out to him, "Peewaubik—Spirit-Iron—Twee! Twee!"

The dog soon came into the lodge, and she set before him the dish of grape-juice.

"See, my child," she said, addressing him, "the pretty drink your mother gives you."

Spirit-Iron took a long draught, and immediately left the lodge with his eyes wide open; for it was the drink which teaches one to see the truth of things as they are. He rose up when he got into the open air, stood upon his hind-legs, and looked about. "I see how it is," he said; and marching off, erect like a man, he sought out his young master.

Approaching him in great confidence, he bent down and whispered in his ear (having first looked cautiously around to see that no one was listening), "This old woman here in the lodge is no mother of yours. I have found your real mother, and she is worth looking at. When we come back from our day's sport, I'll prove it to you."

They went out into the woods, and at the close of the afternoon they brought back a great spoil of meat of all kinds. The young man, as soon as he had laid aside his weapons, said to the old Toad-Woman, "Send some of the best of this meat to the stranger who has arrived lately."

The Toad-Woman answered, "No! Why should I send to her, the poor widow!"

The young man would not be refused; and at last the old Toad-Woman consented to take something and throw it down at the door. She called out, "My son gives you this." But, being bewitched by Mukakee Mindemoea, it was so bitter and distasteful, that the young woman immediately cast it out of the lodge after her.

In the evening the young man paid the stranger a visit at her lodge of cedar-boughs. She then told him that she was his real mother, and that he had been stolen away from her by the old Toad-Woman, who was a child-thief and a witch. As the young man appeared to doubt, she added, "Feign yourself sick when you go home to her lodge; and when the Toad-Woman asks what ails you, say that you wish to see your cradle; for your cradle was of wampum, and your faithful brother the dog, in striving to save you, tore off these pieces which I show you."

They were real wampum, white and blue, shining and beautiful ; and the young man, placing them in his bosom, set off ; but as he did not seem quite steady in his belief of the strange woman's story, the dog Spirit-Iron, taking his arm, kept close by his side, and gave him many words of encouragement as they went along. They entered the lodge together ; and the old Toad-Woman saw, from something in the dog's eye, that trouble was coming.

"Mother," said the young man, placing his hand to his head, and leaning heavily upon Spirit-Iron, as if a sudden faintness had come upon him, "why am I so different in looks from the rest of your children ?"

"Oh," she answered, "it was a very bright, clear blue sky when you were born; that is the reason."

He seemed to be so very ill that the Toad-Woman at length asked what she could do for him. He said nothing could do him good but the sight of his cradle. She ran immediately and brought a cedar cradle; but he said:

"That is not my cradle."

She went and got another of her own children's cradles, of which there were four; but he turned his head, and said:

"That is not mine; I am as sick as ever."

When she had shown the four, and they had been all rejected, she at last produced the real cradle

The young man saw that it was of the same stuff as the wampum which he had in his bosom. He could even see the marks of the teeth of Spirit-Iron left upon the edges, where he had taken hold, striving to hold it back. He had no doubt, now, which was his mother.

To get free of the old Toad-Woman, it was necessary that the young man should kill a fat bear; and, being directed by Spirit-Iron, who was very wise in such a matter, he secured the fattest in all that country; and having stripped a tall pine of all its bark and branches, he perched the carcass in the top, with its head to the east and its tail due west. Returning to the lodge, he informed the old Toad-Woman that the fat bear was ready for her, but that she would have to go very far, even to the end of the earth, to get it. She answered:

" It is not so far but that I can get it;" for of all things in the world, a fat bear was the delight of the old Toad-Woman.

She at once set forth; and she was no sooner out of sight than the young man and his dog, Spirit-Iron, blowing a strong breath in the face of the Toad-Woman's four children (who were all bad spirits, or bear-fiends), they put out their life. They then set them up by the side of the door, having first thrust a piece of the white fat in each of their mouths.

The Toad-Woman spent a long time in finding

the bear which she had been sent after, and she made at least five and twenty attempts before she was able to climb to the carcass. She slipped down three times where she went up once. When she returned with the great bear on her back, as she drew near her lodge she was astonished to see the four children standing up by the door-posts with the fat in their mouths. She was angry with them, and called out:

"Why do you thus insult the pomatum of your brother?"

She was still more angry when they made no answer to her complaint; but when she found that they were stark dead, and placed in this way to mock her, her fury was very great indeed. She ran after the tracks of the young man and his mother as fast as she could; so fast, indeed, that she was on the very point of overtaking them, when the dog, Spirit-Iron, coming close up to his master, whispered to him—"Snakeberry!"

"Let the snakeberry spring up to detain her!" cried out the young man; and immediately the berries spread like scarlet all over the path, for a long distance; and the old Toad-Woman, who was almost as fond of these berries as she was of fat bears, could not avoid stooping down to pick and eat.

The old Toad-Woman was very anxious to get forward, but the snakeberry-vines kept spreading out on every side; and they still grow and grow, and spread and spread; and to this day the wicked old Toad-Woman is busy picking the berries, and she will never be able to get beyond to the other side, to disturb the happiness of the young hunter and his mother, who still live, with their faithful dog, in the shadow of the beautiful wood-side where they were born.

5

IX.

THE ORIGIN OF THE ROBIN

AN old man had an only son, named Iadilla, who had come to that age which is thought to be most proper to make the long and final fast which is to secure through life a guardian genius or spirit. The father was ambitious that his son should surpass all others in whatever was deemed wisest and greatest among his people. To accomplish his wish, he thought it necessary that the young Iadilla should fast a much longer time than any of those renowned for their power or wisdom, whose fame he coveted.

He therefore directed his son to prepare with great ceremony for the important event. After he had been several times in the sweating-lodge and bath, which were to prepare and purify him for communion with his good spirit, he ordered him to lie down upon a clean mat in a little lodge expressly provided for him. He enjoined upon him at the same time to endure his fast like a man, and promised that at the expiration of twelve days he should receive food and the blessing of his father.

The lad carefully observed the command, and lay with his face covered, calmly awaiting the approach of the spirit which was to decide his good or evil fortune for all the days of his life.

Every morning his father came to the door of the little lodge and encouraged him to persevere, dwelling at length on the vast honor and renown that must ever attend him, should he accomplish the full term of trial allotted to him.

To these glowing words of promise and glory the boy never replied, but he lay without the least sign of discontent or murmuring until the ninth day, when he addressed his father as follows:

" My father, my dreams forbode evil. May I break my fast now, and at a more favorable time make a new fast?"

The father answered:

" My son, you know not what you ask. If you get up now, all your glory will depart. Wait patiently a little longer. You have but three days more, and your term will be completed. You know it is for your own good, and I encourage you to persevere. Shall not your aged father live to see you a star among the chieftains and the beloved of battle?"

The son assented; and covering himself more closely, that he might shut out the light which prompted him to complain, he lay till the eleventh day, when he repeated his request.

The father addressed Iadilla as he had the day before, and promised that he would himself prepare his
first meal, and bring it to him by the dawn of the
morning.

The son moaned, and the father added:

" Will you bring shame upon your father when his
sun is falling in the west?"

" I will not shame you, my father," replied Iadilla; and he lay so still and motionless that you
could only know that he was living by the gentle
heaving of his breast.

At the spring of day, the next morning, the father,
delighted at having gained his end, prepared a repast
for his son, and hastened to set it before him. On
coming to the door of the little lodge, he was surprised to hear his son talking to himself. He stooped
his ear to listen, and, looking through a small opening, he was yet more astonished when he beheld his
son painted with vermilion over all his breast, and
in the act of finishing his work by laying on the
paint as far back on his shoulders as he could reach
with his hands, saying at the same time, to himself :

" My father has destroyed my fortune as a man.
He would not listen to my requests. He has urged
me beyond my tender strength. He will be the loser.
I shall be forever happy in my new state, for I have
been obedient to my parent. He alone will be the
sufferer, for my guardian spirit is a just one

Though not propitious to me in the manner I desired, he has shown me pity in another way—he has given me another shape; and now I must go."

At this moment the old man broke in, exclaiming:

"My son! my son! I pray you leave me not!"

But the young man, with the quickness of a bird, had flown to the top of the lodge and perched himself on the highest pole, having been changed into a beautiful robin red-breast. He looked down upon his father with pity beaming in his eyes, and addressed him as follows:

"Regret not, my father, the change you behold. I shall be happier in my present state than I could have been as a man. I shall always be the friend of men, and keep near their dwellings. I shall ever be happy and contented; and although I could not gratify your wishes as a warrior, it will be my daily aim to make you amends for it as a harbinger of peace and joy. I will cheer you by my songs, and strive to inspire in others the joy and lightsomeness of heart I feel in my present state. This will be some compensation to you for the loss of glory you expected. I am now free from the cares and pains of human life. My food is spontaneously furnished by the mountains and fields, and my pathway of life is in the bright air."

Then stretching himself on his toes, as if delighted with the gift of wings, Iadilla caroled one of his sweetest songs, and flew away into a neighboring wood.

X.

WHITE FEATHER AND THE SIX GIANTS.

THERE was an old man living in the depth of a forest, with his grandson, whom he had taken in charge when quite an infant. The child had no parents, brothers, or sisters; they had all been destroyed by six large giants, and he had been informed that he had no other relative living beside his grandfather. The band to whom he had belonged had put up their children on a wager in a race against those of the giants, and had thus lost them. There was an old tradition in the tribe, that, one day, it would produce a great man, who would wear a white feather, and who would astonish every one by his feats of skill and bravery.

The grandfather, as soon as the child could play about, gave him a bow and arrows to amuse himself with. He went into the edge of the woods one day, and saw a rabbit; but not knowing what it was, he ran home and described it to his grandfather. He told him what it was, that its flesh was good to eat, and that if he would shoot one of his arrows into its body he would kill it. The boy went out again and brought home the little animal, which he asked his grandfather to boil, that they might feast on it. He humored the boy in this, and he encouraged him to go on in acquiring the knowledge of hunting, until he could kill deer and the larger kinds of game ; and he became, as he grew up, an expert hunter.

As they lived alone, and away from other Indians, the curiosity of the stripling was excited to know what was passing in the world. One day he came to the edge of a prairie, where he saw ashes like those at his grandfather's lodge, and lodge-poles left standing.

He returned, and inquired whether his grandfather had put up the poles and made the fire. He was answered, No. Nor did he believe that he had seen any thing of the kind. He must have lost his senses to be talking of such things.

Another day the young man went out to see what there was, within a day's hunt, that was curious ; and on entering the woods he heard a voice calling out to him, " Come here, you destined wearer of the White Feather. You do not wear it, yet, but you are worthy of it. Return home and take a short nap. You will dream of hearing a voice, which will tell you to rise and smoke. You will see in your dream a pipe, a smoking-sack, and a large white feather. When you awake you will find these articles. Put the feather on your head, and you will become a great hunter, a great warrior, and a great man, able to do any thing. As a proof that these things shall come to pass, when you smoke, the smoke will turn into pigeons."

The voice then informed the young man who he was, and made known the character of his grandfather, who was imposing upon him to serve his own ends.

The voice-spirit then caused a vine to be laid at his side, and told him that he was now of an age to avenge the wrongs of his kindred. " When you meet your enemy," the spirit added, " you will run a race with him. He will not see the vine, because it is enchanted. While you are running, you will throw it over his head and entangle him, so that you will win the race."

Long before this speech was ended the young man had turned to the quarter from which the voice proceeded, and he was astonished to behold a man ; for as yet he had never seen any human being beside his grandfather.

As he looked more keenly, he saw that this man, who had the looks of great age, was wood from the breast downward, and that he appeared to be fixed in the earth. As his eye dwelt upon this strange being, the countenance by degrees faded away, and when he advanced to the spot whence it had addressed him, it was gone.

He returned home ; slept ; in the midst of his
slumbers, as from the hollow of the air, heard the
voice ; wakened and found the promised gifts. His
grandfather, when his attention was called to his
awakening, was greatly surprised to find the youth
with a white feather on his forehead, and to see flocks
of pigeons flying out of his lodge. He then remembered the old tradition, and knowing that now the
day when he should lose control of his charge had
begun, he bitterly bewailed the hour.

Possessed of his three magic gifts, the young man
departed the next morning, to seek his enemies, and
to demand revenge.

The six giants lived in a very high lodge in the
middle of a wood. He traveled on, in good heart,
till he reached this lodge, where he found that his
coming had been made known by the little spirits
who carry the news. The giants hastened out, and
gave a cry of joy as they saw him drawing near.
When he approached within hail, they began to make
sport of him, saying, "Here comes the little man
with the white feather, who is to achieve such wonderful wonders."

When, however, he had arrived among them, they
spoke him fair, saying he was a brave man and
would do brave things. Their object was to encourage him, so that he would be bold to engage in some
fool-hardy trial of strength.

Without paying much heed to their fine speeches, White Feather went fearlessly into their lodge ; and without waiting for invitation, he challenged them tc a foot-match. They agreed ; and, as they said, by way of being easy with him, they told him to begin the race with the smallest of their number.

The point to which they were to run was a peeled tree toward the rising sun, and then back to the starting-place, which was a war-club of iron. Whoever won this stake, was empowered to use it in dispatching the defeated champion. If White Feather should overcome the first giant, he was to try the second, and so on, until they had all measured speed with him. By a dexterous use of the vine, he gained the first race, struck down his competitor, and cut off his head.

The next morning he ran with the second giant, whom he also outran, killed and beheaded.

He went on in this way for the five mornings, always conquering by the aid of his vine, and lopping off the heads of the vanquished giants.

The last of the giants who was yet to run with him acknowledged his power, but prepared secretly to deceive him. By way of parley, he proposed that White Feather should leave the heads with him, and that he would give him a handsome start for odds. This White Feather declined, as he preferred to keep the heads as trophies of his victory.

Before going to the giant's lodge, on the sixth morning, he met his old counselor in the woods, standing rooted in the earth, as before. He told White Feather that he was about to be deceived; that he had never known any other sex but his own, but that as he went on his way to the lodge he would meet the most beautiful woman in the world. He must pay no attention to her, but as soon as he caught her eye he must wish himself changed into an elk. The change would take place immediately, and he must go to feeding and not look at her again.

White Feather thanked his kind adviser, and when he turned to take his leave he was gone as before.

He proceeded toward the lodge, met the female as had been foretold to him, and became an elk. She reproached him that he had cast aside the form of a man that he might avoid her.

"I have traveled a great distance," she added, "to see you and to become your wife; for I have heard of your great achievements, and admire you very much."

Now this woman was the sixth giant, who had assumed this disguise to entrap White Feather.

Without a suspicion of her real character, her reproaches and her beauty affected him so deeply that he wished himself a man again, and he at once resumed his natural shape. They sat down together, and he began to caress and to make love to her.

Soothed by her smiles and her gracious manners, he ventured to lay his head on her lap, and in a little while he fell into a deep slumber.

Even then, such was her fear of White Feather, she doubted whether his sleep might not be feigned. To assure herself she pushed his head aside, and seeing that he remained unconscious, she quickly assumed her own form as the sixth giant, took the plume from the brow of White Feather and placed it upon his own head, and with a sudden blow of his war-club changed him into a dog, in which degraded form he followed his enemy to the lodge.

While these things were passing, there were living in an Indian village at some distance, two sisters, the daughters of a chief, who were rivals, and they were at that very time fasting to acquire power, for the purpose of enticing the wearer of the white feather to visit their lodge. They each secretly hoped to engage his affections, and each had built a lodge in the border of the village encampment.

The giant knowing this, and having become possessed of the magic plume, went immediately to visit them. As he approached, the sisters, who were on the look-out at their lodge-doors, espied and recognized the feather.

The eldest sister had prepared her lodge with great show, and all the finery she could command, so as to attract the eye. The youngest touched nothing in her lodge, but left it in its ordinary state.

The eldest went out to meet the giant, and invited him in. He accepted her invitation, and made her his wife. The youngest sister invited the enchanted dog into her lodge, prepared him a good supper and a neat bed, and treated him with much attention.

The giant, supposing that whoever possessed the white feather possessed also all its virtues, went out upon the prairie to hunt, hallooing aloud to the game to come and be killed; but the great hubbub he kept up scared them away, and he returned at night with nothing but himself; for he had shouted so lustily all day long that he had been even obliged to leave the mighty halloo, with which he had set out, behind.

The dog went out the same day hunting upon the banks of a river. He stole quietly along to the spot, and stepping into the water he drew out a stone, which instantly became a beaver.

The next day the giant followed the dog, and hiding behind a tree, he watched the manner in which the dog hunted in the river when he drew out a stone, which at once turned into a beaver.

" Ah, ha!" said the giant to himself, " I will catch some beaver for myself."

And as soon as the dog had left the place, the giant went to the river, and, imitating the dog, he drew out a stone, and was delighted to see it, as soon as it touched the land, change into a fine fat beaver.

Tying it to his belt he hastened home, shouting a good deal, and brandishing the white feather about, as if he were prepared now to show them what he could do when he once tried. When he reached home he threw it down, as is the custom, at the door of the lodge before he entered.

After being seated a short time, he gave a dry cough, and bade his wife bring in his hunting girdle. She made dispatch to obey him, and presently returned with the girdle, with nothing tied to it but a stone.

The next day, the dog finding that his method of catching beavers had been discovered, went to a wood at some distance, and broke off a charred limb from a burned tree, which instantly became a bear. The giant, who appeared to have lost faith in his hulla-balooing, had again watched him, did exactly as the dog had done, and carried a bear home ; but his wife, when she came to go out for it, found nothing but a black stick tied to his belt.

And so it happened with every thing. Whatever the dog undertook, prospered ; whatever the giant attempted, failed. Every day the youngest sister had reason to be more proud of the poor dog she had asked into her lodge, and every day the eldest sister was made more aware, that though she had married the white feather, the virtues of the magic plume were not the personal property of the noisy giant.

At last the giant's wife determined that she would go to her father and make known to him what a valuable husband she had, and how he furnished her lodge with a great abundance of sticks and stones, which he would pass upon her for bear and beaver. So, when her husband, whose brave halloo had now died away to a feeble chirp, had started for the hunt, she set out.

As soon as these two had gone away from the neighborhood, the dog made signs to his mistress to sweat him after the manner of the Indians. He had always been a good dog, and she was willing to oblige him. She accordingly made a lodge just large enough for him to creep in. She then put in heated stones, and poured water upon them, which raised a vapor that filled the lodge and searched with its warmth to the very heart's core of the enchanted dog.

When this had been kept up for the customary time, the enchanted dog was completely sweated away, and in his stead, as might have been expected, out came a very handsome young man, but, unhappily, without the power of speech. In taking away the dog, it appears that the sweating-lodge had also carried off the voice with it.

Meantime the elder sister had reached her father's,

and, with much circumstance and a very long face, had told him how that her sister was supporting an idle dog, and entertaining him as her husband. In her anxiety to make known her sister's affairs and the great scandal she was bringing upon the family, the eldest forgot to say any thing of the sticks and stones which her own husband brought home for bears and beavers. The old man suspecting that there was magic about her house, sent a deputation of young men and women to ask his youngest daughter to come to him, and to bring her dog along with her. When the deputation reached the lodge, they were surprised to find, in the place of the dog, a fine young man ; and on announcing their message, they all returned to the old chief, who was no less surprised at the change.

He immediately assembled all the old and wise heads of the nation to come and be witnesses to the exploits which it was reported that the young man could perform. The sixth giant, although neither very old nor very wise, thrust himself in among the relations of the old chief.

When they were all assembled and seated in a circle, the old chief took his pipe and filled it, and passed it to the Indians around, to see if any thing would happen when they smoked. They passed it on until it came around to the Dog, who made a sign that it should be handed first to the giant, which was done. And the giant puffed with all his might, and shook the white feather upon his head, and swelled his chest; but nothing came of it, except a great deal of smoke. The Dog then took it himself. He made a sign to them to put the white feather upon his head. This was no sooner done, than he recovered his speech, and, beginning to draw upon the pipe at the same moment, behold, immense flocks of white and blue pigeons rushed from the smoke.

From that moment the sixth giant was looked upon as an impostor, and as soon as White Feather had, at the request of the company, faithfully recounted his history, the old chief, who was one of the best-hearted magicians that ever lived, ordered that the giant should be transformed into a dog, and turned into the middle of the village, where the boys should pelt him to death with clubs; which being done, the whole six giants were at an end, and never troubled that neighborhood again, forever after.

The chief then gave out a command, at the request of White Feather, that all the young men should employ themselves four days in making arrows. White Feather also asked for a buffalo robe. This he cut into thin shreds, and in the night, when no one knew of it, he went and sowed them about the prairie in every direction.

At the end of the four days, he invited them to gather together all of their arrows, and to accompany him to a buffalo hunt. When they got out upon the prairie, they found it covered with a great herd of buffaloes. Of these they killed as many as they pleased, and, afterward, they had a grand festival in honor of White Feather's triumph over the giants.

All this being pleasantly over, White Feather got his wife to ask her father's permission to go with him on a visit to his grandfather. The old chief replied to this application, that a woman must follow her husband into whatever quarter of the world he may choose to go.

Bidding farewell to all his friends, White Feather placed the plume in his frontlet, and taking his war-club in his hand, he led the way into the forest, followed by his faithful wife.

XI.

SHEEM, THE FORSAKEN BOY.

ON a certain afternoon the sun was falling in the West, and in the midst of the ruddy silence a solitary lodge stood on the banks of a remote lake. One sound only broke, in the least degree, the forest stillness—the low breathing of the dying inmate, who was the head of a poor family. His wife and children surrounded the buffalo robe on which he lay. Of the children, two were almost grown up—a daughter and a son ; the other was a boy, and a mere child in years.

All the skill of the household in their simple medicines was exhausted, and they stood looking on or moved about the lodge with whispered steps, awaiting the departure of the spirit. As one of the last acts of kindness, the skin door of the lodge had been thrown back to admit the fresh air of the evening. The poor man felt a momentary return of strength, and raising himself a little, he addressed his family.

"I leave you," he said, "in a world of care, in which it has required all my strength and skill to supply you food, and to protect you from the storms and cold of a harsh climate."

He cast his eyes upon his wife, and continued:

" For you, my partner in life, I have less sorrow, because I am persuaded you will not remain long behind me; but you, my children! my poor and forsaken children, who have just begun the career of life, who will shelter you from calamity? Listen to my words. Unkindness, ingratitude, and every wickedness, are in the scene before you. It was for this that years ago I withdrew from my kindred and my tribe to spend my days in this lonely spot. I have contented myself with the company of your mother and yourselves, during seasons of very frequent scarcity and want, while your kindred, feasting in plenty, have caused the forests to echo with the shouts of successful war. I gave up these things for the enjoyment of peace. I wished to hide you away from the bad examples which would have spoiled your innocence. I have seen you, thus far, grow up in purity of heart. If we have sometimes suffered bodily want. we have escaped pain of mind. We have not been compelled to look on or to take a part with the red hand in scenes of rioting and bloodshed. My path now stops. I have arrived at the brink of the world. I will shut my eyes in peace if you, my children, will promise me to cherish each other. Let not your mother suffer during the few days that are left to her; and I charge you, on no account, to forsake your younger brother. Of him I give you both my dying command to have a tender care."

He spoke no more, and as the sun fell out of view the light had gone from his face. The family stood still, as if they expected to hear something further; but when they came to his side and called him by name, his spirit did not answer. It was in another world.

The mother and daughter lamented aloud, but the elder son clothed himself in silence, as though it had been a mantle, and took his course as though nothing had occurred. He exerted himself to supply, with his bow and net, the wants of the little household, but he never made mention of his father.

Five moons had filled and waned, and the sixth was near its full, when the mother also died. In her last moments she pressed the fulfillment of their father's wish.

The winter passed, and the spring, sparkling in the clear northern air, cheered the spirits of the lonely little people in the lodge.

The girl, being the eldest, directed her brothers, and she seemed to feel a tender and sisterly affection for the youngest, who was slight in frame and of a delicate temper. The other boy soon began to break forth with restless speeches, which showed that his spirit was not at ease. One day he addressed his sister as follows :

" My sister, are we always to live as if there were no other human beings in the world ? Must I deprive myself of the pleasure of mingling with my own kind ? I have determined this question for myself. I shall seek the villages of men, and you can not prevent me."

The sister replied :

" I do not say no, my brother, to what you desire; we are not forbidden the society of our fellow-mortals, but we are told to cherish each other, and to do nothing that shall not be agreeable to all our little household. Neither pleasure nor pain ought, therefore, to separate us, especially from our younger brother, who, being but a child, and weakly withal, is entitled to a double share of our affection. If we follow our separate fancies, it will surely make us neglect him, whom we are bound by vows, both to our father and mother, to support."

The young man received this address in silence, and still took his course as though nothing out of the ordinary way had occurred. After awhile he seemed to recover his spirits; and as they lived in a large country, where there were open fields, the two brothers, at his invitation, often amused themselves in playing ball. One afternoon he chose the ground near to a beautiful lake, and they played and laughed with great spirit, and the ball was seldom allowed to touch the ground.

Now in this lake there happened to harbor a wicked old Manito, Mishosha by name, who looked at the brothers as they played, and he was vastly pleased with their nimbleness and beauty. He thought to himself, what shall I do to get these lads to accompany me ? One of them shall hit the ball sideways, and it shall fall into my canoe.

It so happened, and it somehow seemed as if Owasso, the elder brother, had purposely given it that direction. When Owasso saw the old man, he professed to be greatly surprised, as was the other, Sheem by name, in truth, for he had not noticed the old Manito before.

"Bring the ball to us," they both cried out. "Come to the shore."

"No," answered the old magician. He, however, came near enough for either of them to wade out to him. "Come, come," he said. "Come and get your ball."

They insisted that he should come ashore, but he sturdily declined to oblige them.

"Very well," said Owasso, "I will go and get it." And he ran into the water. "Hand it to me," he said, when he had approached near enough to receive it.

"Ha!" answered the Manito, "reach over and get it yourself."

Owasso was about to grasp the ball, when the old magician suddenly seized him and pushed him into the boat.

"My grandfather," said Owasso, "pray take my little brother also. Alone I can not go with you; he will starve if I leave him."

Mishosha only laughed at him; then uttering the charmed words, "Chemaun Poll!" and giving his canoe a slap, it glided through the water, without further help, with the swiftness of an arrow.

In a short time they reached the magician's lodge, which stood upon the further shore, a little distance back from the lake. The two daughters of Mishosha were seated within. "My daughter," he said to his eldest, as they entered the lodge, "I have brought you a husband."

The young woman smiled; for Owasso was a comely youth to look upon. The magician told him to take his seat near her, and by this act the marriage ceremony was completed, and Owasso and the magician's daughter were man and wife, and in the course of time they had born to them a son.

But no sooner was Owasso in the family than the old Manito wished him out of the way, and he went about in his own wicked fashion to compass it.

One day he asked his son-in-law to go out a-fish-

ing with him. They started without delay ; for the
magician had only to speak, and off went the canoe.
They reached a solitary bay in an island, a very dark,
lonely, and out-of-the-way place. The Manito advised Owasso to spear a large sturgeon which came
alongside, and with its great glassy eye turned up,
seemed to recognize the magician. Owasso rose in
the boat to dart his spear, and by speaking that moment to his canoe, Mishosha shot forward and hurled
his son-in-law headlong into the water; where, leaving him to struggle for himself, he was soon out of
sight.

Owasso, being himself gifted with limited magical
powers, spoke to the fish, and bade him swim toward
the lodge, while he carried him along, which he did
at great speed. Once he directed the sturgeon to rise
near the surface of the water, so that he might, if
possible, get a view of the magician. The fish
obeyed, and Owasso saw the wicked old Manito busy
in another direction, fishing, as unconcerned as
though he had not just lost a member of his
family.

On went the fish, and on went Owasso, till they
reached the shore, near the magician's lodge, in advance of him. He then spoke kindly to the sturgeon, and told him he should not be angry with him
for having speared him, as he was created to be meat
for man. The sturgeon made no reply, or if he did,

6

it has not been reported ; and Owasso, drawing him
on shore, went up and told his wife to dress and cook
it immediately. By the time it was prepared the
magician had come in sight.

"Your grandfather has arrived," said the woman
to her son ; "go and see what he brings, and eat this
as you go "—handing a piece of the fish.

The boy went, and the magician no sooner saw
him with the fish in his hand, than he asked him,
"What are you eating ? and who brought it ?"

He replied, "My father brought it."

The magician began to feel uneasy, for he found
that he had been outwitted ; he, however, put on a
grave face, and entering the lodge, acted as if nothing
unusual had happened.

Some days after this, Mishosha again requested his
son-in-law to accompany him ; and Owasso, without
hesitation, said "Yes !"

They went out, and, in a rapid passage, they arrived at a solitary island, which was no more than a
heap of high and craggy rocks.

The magician said to Owasso, "Go on shore, my
son, and pick up all the gulls' eggs you can find."

The rocks were strewn with eggs, and the air resounded with the cry of the birds as they saw them
gathered up by Owasso.

The old magician took the opportunity to speak to
the gulls. "I have long wished," he said, "to offer

you something. I now give you this young man for
food."

He then uttered the charm to his canoe, and it shot
out of sight, leaving Owasso to make his peace the
best way he could.

The gulls flew in immense numbers around him,
and were ready to devour him. Owasso did not lose
his presence of mind, but he addressed them and said :

" Gulls, you know you were not formed to eat human flesh, nor was man made to be the prey of birds.
Obey my words. Fly close together, a sufficient
number of you, and carry me on your backs to the
magician's lodge."

They listened attentively to what he said, and seeing nothing unreasonable in his request, they obeyed
him, and Owasso soon found himself sailing through
the air swiftly homeward.

Meanwhile, it appears that the old magician had
fallen asleep and allowed his canoe to come to a
stand-still; for Owasso, in his flight over the lake,
saw him lying on his back in the boat, taking a nap,
which was quite natural, as the day was very soft and
balmy.

As Owasso, with his convoy of birds, passed over,
he let fall, directly in the face of the old magician, a
capful of gulls' eggs, which broke and so besmeared
his eyes that he could barely see. He jumped up and
exclaimed :

"It is always so with these thoughtless birds. They never consider where they drop their eggs."

Owasso had flown on and reached the lodge in safety, and, excusing himself for the liberty, he killed two or three of the gulls for the sake of their feathers to ornament his son's head.

When the magician arrived, soon after, his grandson came out to meet him, tossing his head about as the feathers danced and struggled with the wind.

"Where did you get these?" asked the Manito, "and who brought them?"

"My father brought them," the boy replied.

The old magician was quite distressed in his mind that he had not destroyed his son-in-law. He entered his lodge in silence, and set his wits busily at work again to contrive some plan for easing his feelings in that respect.

He could not help saying to himself:

"What manner of boy is this who is ever escaping from my power? But his guardian spirit shall not save him. I will entrap him to-morrow. Ha, ha, ha!"

He was painfully aware that he had tried two of his charms without effect, and that he had but two more left. He now professed to be more friendly with his son-in-law than ever, and the very next day he said to Owasso:

"Come, my son, you must go with me to procure

some young eagles. We will tame them, and have them for pets about the lodge. I have discovered an islan l where they are in great abundance."

They started on the trip, and when, after traversing an immense waste of water, they had reached the island, Mishosha led him inland until they came to the foot of a tall pine-tree, upon which the nests were to be found.

"Now, my son," said Mishosha, "climb up this tree and bring down the birds. I think you will get some fine ones up there."

Owasso obeyed. When he had with great difficulty got near the nest, Mishosha cried out, addressing himself to the tree, and without much regard to the wishes of Owasso :

"Now stretch yourself up and be very tall."

The tree, at this bidding, rose up so far that Owasso would have imperiled his neck by any attempt to get to the ground.

"Listen, ye eagles !" continued Mishosha. "You have long expected a gift from me. I now present you this boy, who has had the presumption to climb up where you are to molest your young. Stretch forth your claws and seize him."

So saying, the old magician, according to his custom in such cases, turned his back upon Owasso, and going off in his canoe at a word, he left his son-in-law to shift for himself.

But the birds did not seem to be so badly-minded as the old magician had supposed; for a very old bald eagle, quite corpulent and large of limb, alighting on a branch just opposite, opened conversation with him by asking what had brought him there.

Owasso replied that he had not mounted the tree of himself, or out of any disposition to harm his people; that his father-in-law, the old magician who had just left them, had sent him up; that he was constantly sending him on mischievous errands. In a word, the young man was enlarging at great length upon the character of the wicked Manito, when he was interrupted by being darted upon by a hungry-eyed bird, with long claws.

Owasso, not in the least disconcerted, boldly seized this fierce eagle by the neck and dashed it against the rocks, crying out:

"Thus will I deal with all who come near me."

The old eagle, who appeared to be the head of the tribe, was so pleased with this show of spirit that he immediately appointed two tall birds, uncommonly strong in the wings, to transport Owasso to his lodge. They were to take turns in conducting him through the air,

Owasso expressed many obligations to the old eagle for his kindness, and they forthwith set out. It was a high point from which they started, for the pine-tree had shot far, far up toward the clouds, and they

could even descry the enchanted island where the old
magician lived; though it was miles and miles away.
For this point they steered their flight; and in a
short time they landed Owasso at the door of the
lodge.

With many compliments for their dispatch, Owasso
dismissed the birds, and stood ready to greet his
wicked father-in-law who now arrived; and when he
espied his son-in-law still unharmed, Mishosha grew
very black in the face. He had but a single charm
left.

He thought he would ponder deeply how he could
employ that to the best advantage; and it happened
that while he was doing so, one evening, as Owasso
and his wife were sitting on the banks of the lake,
and the soft breeze swept over it, they heard a song,
as if sung by some one at a great distance. The
sound continued for some time, and then died away
in perfect stillness. "Oh, it is the voice of Sheem,"
cried Owasso. "It is the voice of my brother! If I
could but only see him!" And he hung down his
head in deep anguish.

His wife witnessed his distress, and to comfort him
she proposed that they should attempt to make their
escape, and carry him succor on the morrow.

When the morning came, and the sun shone
warmly into the lodge, the wife of Owasso offered to
comb her father's hair, with the hope that it would

soothe him to sleep. It had that effect; and they no sooner saw him in deep slumber than they seized the magic canoe, and Owasso uttering the charmed words, *Chemaun Poll!* they glided away upon the water without need of oar or sail.

They had nearly reached the land on the opposite side of the lake, and could distinctly hear the voice of the younger brother singing his lament as before, when the old magician wakened. Missing his daughter and her husband, he suspected deception of some kind; he looked for his magic boat and found it gone. He spoke the magic words, which were more powerful from him than from any other person in the world, and the canoe immediately returned; to the sore disappointment of Owasso and his wife.

When they came back to the shore, Mishosha stood upon the beach and drew up his canoe. He did not utter a word. The son-in-law and daughter entered the lodge in silence.

The time, walking along in its broad open path, brought the autumn months to a close, and the winter had set in. Soon after the first fall of snow, Owasso said, "Father, I wish to try my skill in hunting. It is said there is plenty of game not far off, and it can now be easily tracked. Let us go."

The magician consented; they set out, and arriving at a good ground for their sport, they spent the day in hunting. Night coming on, they built themselves a lodge of pine-branches to sleep in. Although it was bitterly cold, the young man took off his leggings and moccasins, and hung them up to dry. The old magician did the same, carefully hanging his own n a separate place, and they lay down to sleep.

Owasso, from a glance he had given, suspected that the magician had a mind to play him a trick, and to be beforehand with him, he watched an opportunity to get up and change the moccasins and leggings, putting his own in the place of Mishosha's, and depending on the darkness of the lodge to help him through.

Near daylight, the old magician bestirred himself, as if to rekindle the fire ; but he slyly reached down a pair of moccasins and leggings with a stick, and thinking they were no other than those of Owasso's, he dropped them into the flames ; while he cast himself down, and affected to be lost in a heavy sleep. The leather leggings and moccasins soon drew up and were burned.

Instantly jumping up and rubbing his eyes, Mishosha cried out:

" Son-in-law, your moccasins are burning ; I know it by the smell."

Owasso rose up, deliberately and unconcerned.

" No, my friend," said he, " here are mine," at the same time taking them down and drawing them on.

" It is your moccasins that are burning."

Mishosha dropped his head upon his breast. **All** his tricks were played out—there was not so much as half a one left to help him out of the sorry plight he was in.

" I believe, my grandfather," added Owasso, " that this is the moon in which fire attracts, and I fear you must have set your foot and leg garments too near the fire, and they have been drawn in. Now let us go forth to the hunt."

The old magician was compelled to follow him, and they pushed out into a great storm of snow, and hail, and wind, which had come on over night; and neither the wind, the hail, nor the snow, had the slightest respect for the bare limbs of the old magician, for there was not the least virtue of magic in those parts of old Mishosha's body. After a while they quite stiffened under him, his body became hard, and the hair bristled in the cold wind, so that he looked to Owasso—who turned away from him, leaving the wicked old magician alone to ponder upon his past life—to Owasso he looked like a tough old sycamore-tree more than a highly-gifted old ma-gician.

Owasso himself reached home in safety, proof against all kinds of weather, and the magic canoe became the exclusive property of the young man and his wife.

During all this part of Owasso's stay at the lodge

of Mishosha, his sister, whom he had left on the main land with Sheem, their younger brother, had labored with good-will to supply the lodge. She knew enough of the arts of the forest to provide their daily food, and she watched her little brother, and tended his wants, with all of a good sister's care. By times she began to be weary of solitude and of her charge. No one came to be a witness of her constancy, or to let fall a single word in her mother-tongue. She could not converse with the birds and beasts about her, and she felt, to the bottom of her heart, that she was alone. In these thoughts she forgot her younger brother ; she almost wished him dead ; for it was he alone that kept her from seeking the companionship of others.

One day, after collecting all the provisions she had been able to reserve from their daily use, and bringing a supply of wood to the door, she said to her little brother :

"My brother, you must not stray from the lodge. I am going to seek our elder brother. I shall be back soon."

She then set the lodge in perfect order, and, taking her bundle, she set off in search of habitations. These she soon found, and in the enjoyment of the pleasures and pastimes of her new acquaintance, she began to think less and less of her little brother, Sheem. She accepted proposals of marriage, and from that time she utterly forgot the abandoned boy.

As for poor little Sheem, he was soon brought to the pinching turn of his fate. As soon as he had eaten all of the food left in the lodge, he was obliged to pick berries, and live off of such roots as he could dig with his slender hands. As he wandered about in search of wherewithal to stay his hunger, he often looked up to heaven, and saw the gray clouds going up and down. And then he looked about upon the wide earth, but he never saw sister nor brother returning from their long delay.

At last, even the roots and berries gave out. They were blighted by the frost or hidden out of reach by the snow, for the mid-winter had come on, and poor little Sheem was obliged to leave the lodge and wander away in search of food.

Sometimes he was enforced to pass the night in the clefts of old trees or caverns, and to break his fast with the refuse meals of the savage wolves.

These at last became his only resource, and he grew to be so little fearful of these animals that he would sit by them while they devoured their meat, and patiently await his share.

After a while, the wolves took to little Sheem very kindly, and seeming to understand his outcast condition, they would always leave something for him to eat. By and by they began to talk with him, and to inquire into his history. When he told them that he had been forsaken by his brother and his sister, the wolves turned about to each other, lifted up their eyes to heaven, and wondered among themselves, with raised paws, that such a thing should have been.

In this way, Sheem lived on till the spring, and as soon as the lake was free from ice, he followed his new friends to the shore.

It happened on the same day, that his elder brother, Owasso, was fishing in his magic canoe, a considerable distance out upon the lake ; when he thought he heard the cries of a child upon the shore. He wondered how any human creature could exist on so bleak and barren a coast.

He listened again with all attention, and he heard the cry distinctly repeated ; and this time it was the well-known cry of his younger brother that reached his ear. He knew too well the secret of his song, as he heard him chaunting mournfully:

"My brother! My brother! Since you left me going in the canoe, a-hee-ee, I am half changed into a wolf, E-wee. I am half changed into a wolf, E-wee."

Owasso made for the shore. and as he approached the lament was repeated. The sounds were very distinct, and the voice of wailing was very sorrowful for Owasso to listen to, and it touched him the more that it died away at the close, into a long-drawn howl, like that of the wolf.

In the sand, as he drew closer to the land, he saw the tracks as of that animal fleeing away; and besides these the prints of human hands. But what were the pity and astonishment that smote Owasso to the heart when he espied his poor little brother—poor little forsaken Sheem—half boy and half wolf, flying along the shore.

Owasso immediately leaped upon the ground and strove to catch him in his arms, saying soothingly, " My brother! my brother! Come to me."

But the poor wolf-boy avoided his grasp, crying, as he fled, " Neesia, neesia. Since you left me going in the canoe, a-he-ee, I am half changed into a wolf, E-wee. I am half changed into a wolf, E-wee!" and howling between these words of lament.

The elder brother, sore at heart, and feeling all of his brotherly affection strongly returning, with renewed anguish, cried out, " My brother! my brother! my brother!"

But the nearer he approached to poor Sheem, the faster he fled, and the more rapidly the change went on; the boy-wolf by turns singing and howling, and calling out the name, first of his brother and then of his sister, till the change was complete. He leaped upon a bank, and looking back, and casting upon Owasso a glance of deep reproach and grief, he exclaimed, " I am a wolf!" and disappeared in the woods.

XII.

THE MAGIC BUNDLE.

A POOR man, called Iena, or the Wanderer, was in the habit of roaming about from place to place, forlorn, without relations, and almost helpless. He had often wished for a companion to share his solitude ; but who would think of joining their fortunes with those of a poor wanderer, who had no shelter but such as his leather hunting-shirt provided, and no other household in the world than the bundle which he carried in his hand, and in which his hunting-shirt was laid away?

One day as he went on a hunting excursion, to relieve himself of the burden of carrying it, Iena hung up his bundle on the branch of a tree, and then set out in quest of game.

On returning to the spot in the evening, he was surprised to find a small but neat lodge built in the place where he had left his bundle; and on looking in he beheld a beautiful female, sitting on the further side of the lodge, with his bundle lying beside her.

During the day Iena had so far prospered in his sport as to kill a deer, which he now cast down at the lodge door.

Without pausing to take the least notice, or to give a word of welcome to the hunter, the woman ran out and began to see whether it was a large deer that he had brought. In her haste she stumbled and fell at the threshold.

Iena looked at her with astonishment, and thought to himself, "I supposed I was blessed, but I find my mistake. Night-Hawk," said he, speaking aloud, "I will leave my game with you that you may feast on it."

He then took up his bundle and departed. After walking some time he came to another tree, on which he suspended his bundle as before, and went in search of game.

Success again attended him, and he returned, bringing with him a deer, and he found that a lodge had sprung up as before, where he had hung his bundle. He looked in and saw a beautiful female sitting alone, with his bundle by her side.

She arose and came out toward the deer which he had deposited at the door, and he immediately went into the lodge and sat by the fire, as he was weary with the day's hunt, which had carried him far away.

The woman did not return, and wondering at her delay, Iena at last arose, and peeping through the door of the lodge, beheld her greedily eating all the fat of the deer. He exclaimed, "I thought I was blessed, but I find I was mistaken." Then address-ing the woman : "Poor Marten," said he, "feast on the game I have brought."

He again took up his bundle and departed; and, as usual, hung it upon the branch of a tree, and wandered off in quest of game.

In the evening he returned, with his customary good luck, bringing in a fine deer. He again found that a lodge had taken the place of his bundle. He gazed through an opening in the side of the lodge, and there was another beautiful woman sitting alone, with a bundle by her side.

As soon as he entered the lodge, she rose cheer-fully, welcomed him home, and without delay or complaining, she brought in the deer, cut it up as it should be, and hung up the meat to dry. She then prepared a portion of it for the supper of the weary hunter. The man thought to himself, "Now I am certainly blessed."

He continued his practice of hunting every day, and the woman, on his return, always welcomed him, readily took charge of the meat, and promptly pre-pared his evening meal; and he ever after lived a contented and happy man.

XIII.

THE RED SWAN.

THREE brothers were left destitute, by the **death** of their parents, at an early age. The eldest was not yet able to provide fully for their support, but he did all that he could in hunting; and with this aid, and the stock of provisions already laid by in the lodge, they managed to keep along. They had no neighbors to lend them a helping hand, for the father had withdrawn many years before from the body of the tribe, and had lived ever since in a solitary place. The lads had no idea that there was a human being near them. They did not even know who their parents had been; for, at the time of their death, the eldest was too young to remember it.

Forlorn as they were, they however kept a good heart, and making use of every chance, in course of time they all acquired a knowledge of hunting and the pursuit of game. The eldest became expert in the craft of the forest, and he was very successful in procuring food. He was noted for his skill in killing buffalo, elk, and moose; and he instructed his brothers, so that each should become a master over a particular animal which was assigned to him.

After they had become able to hunt and to take care of themselves, the elder proposed to leave them and to go in search of the world, promising to return as soon as he could procure them wives. In this intention he was overruled by his brothers, who said that they could not part with him.

Jeekewis, the second, was loud in disapproval of the scheme, saying : " What will you do with those you propose to get ? We have lived so long by ourselves, we can still do without them." This counsel prevailed, and for a time the three brothers continued together.

One day they agreed to kill each a male of that kind of animal, which each was most expert in hunting, for the purpose of making quivers from their skins. When these quivers were prepared, they were straightway filled with arrows ; for they all had a presentiment that something was about to happen which called upon them to be ready.

Soon after they hunted on a wager to see who should come in first with game, and have the privilege of acting as entertainer to the others. They were to shoot no other beast or bird than such as each was in the habit of killing.

They set out on different paths. Maidwa, the youngest, had not gone far before he saw a bear, an animal he was not to kill, by the agreement. He, however, followed him closely, and driving an arrow through and through him, he brought him to the ground.

Although contrary to the engagement with his brothers, Maidwa commenced skinning him, when suddenly something red tinged the air all around him. He rubbed his eyes, thinking he was perhaps deceived ; but rub as hard as he would, the red hue still crimsoned the air, and tinged every object that he looked on—the tree-tops, the river that flowed, and the deer that glided away along the edge of the forest—with its delicate splendor.

As he stood musing on this fairy spectacle, a strange noise came to his ear from a distance. At first it seemed like a human voice. After following the sound he reached the shore of a lake. Floating at a distance upon its waters sat a most beautiful Red Swan, whose plumage glittered in the sun, and when it lifted up its neck, it uttered the peculiar tone he had heard. He was within long bow-shot, and, drawing the arrow to his ear, he took a careful aim and discharged the shaft. It took no effect. The beautiful bird sat proudly on the water, still pouring forth its peculiar chant, and still spreading the radiance of its plumage far and wide, and lighting up the whole world, beneath the eye of Maidwa, with its ruby splendors.

He shot again and again, till his quiver was empty, for he longed to possess so glorious a creature. Still the swan did not spread its wings to fly, but, circling round and round, stretched its long neck and dipped its bill into the water, as if indifferent to mortal shafts,

Maidwa ran home, and bringing all the arrows in the lodge, shot them away. He then stood with his bow dropped at his side, lost in wonder, gazing at the beautiful bird.

While standing thus, with a heart beating more and more eagerly every moment for the possession of this fair swan, Maidwa remembered the saying of his elder brother, that in their deceased father's medicine-sack were three magic arrows ; but his brother had not told Maidwa that their father, on his death-bed, which he alone had attended, had especially bequeathed the arrows to his youngest son, Maidwa, from whom they had been wrongfully kept. The thought of the magic arrows put heart in Maidwa, and he hastened with all speed to secure them.

At any other time he would have shrunk from opening his father's medicine-sack, but something prompted him to believe that there was no wrong now, and snatching them forth he ran back, not staying to restore the other contents to the sack, but leaving them scattered, here and there, about the lodge.

He feared, as he returned, that the swan must by this time have taken wing ; but, as he emerged from the wood, to his great delight the air was as rosy as ever, and there, in her own serene and beautiful way, still sat the glorious Red Swan.

With trembling hand he shot the first of his magic shafts : it grazed a wing. The second came closer, and cut away a few of the bright red feathers, which fluttered and fell like flakes of fire in the water. The third, which he carefully aimed and drew home upon the string with all his force, made the lucky hit, and passed through the neck of the bird a little above the breast.

" The bird is mine," said Maidwa, to himself ; but to his great surprise, instead of seeing it droop its neck and drift to the shore, the Red Swan flapped its wings, rose slowly, and flew off with a majestic motion toward the falling sun.

Maidwa, that he might meet his brothers, rescued two of the magic arrows from the water ; and although the third was borne off, he had a hope yet to recover that too, and to be master of the swan. He was noted for his speed ; for he would shoot an arrow and then run so fast that the arrow always fell behind him ; and he now set off at his best speed of foot. " I can run fast," he thought, " and I can get up with the swan some time or other."

He sped on, over hills and prairies, toward the west.

and was only going to take one more run, and then
seek a place to sleep for the night, when, suddenly,
he heard noises at a distance, like the murmur of
waters against the shore ; as he went on, he heard
voices, and presently he saw people, some of whom
were busy felling trees, and the strokes of their labor
echoed through the woods. He passed on, and when
he emerged from the forest, the sun was just falling
below the edge of the sky.

He was bent on success in pursuit of the swan,
whose red track he marked well far westward till she
was lost to sight. Meanwhile he would tarry for the
night and procure something to eat, as he had fasted
since he had left home.

At a distance, on a rising ground, he could see the
lodges of a large village. He went toward it, and
soon heard the watchman, who was set on a height to
overlook the place, and give notice of the approach
of friends or foes, crying out, " We are visited;" and
a loud halloo indicated that they had all heard it.

When Maidwa advanced, the watchman pointed to
the lodge of the chief. " It is there you must go in,"
he said, and left him.

" Come in, come in," said the chief ; " take a seat
there;" pointing to the side of the lodge where his
daughter sat. " It is there you must sit."

They gave him something to eat, and, being a
stranger, very few questions were put to him; it

was only when he spoke that the others answered him.

"Daughter," said the chief, as soon as the night had set in, "take our son-in-law's moccasins and see if they be torn ; if so, mend them for him, and bring in his bundle."

Maidwa thought it strange that he should be so warmly received, and married instantly against his own wishes, although he could not help noticing that the chief's daughter was pretty.

It was some time before she would take the moccasins which he had laid off. It displeased him to see her loth to do so; and when at last she did reach them, he snatched them from her hand and hung them up himself. He lay down and thought of the swan, and made up his mind to be off with the dawn. He wakened early, and finding the chief's daughter looking forth at the door, he spoke to her, but she gave no answer. He touched her lightly.

"What do you want?" she said, and turned her face away from him.

"Tell me," said Maidwa, "what time the swan passed. I am following it; come out, and point the way."

"Do you think you can overtake it?" she said.

"Yes," he answered.

"Naubesah—fool!" retorted the chief's pretty daughter.

She, however, went out, and pointed in the direction he should go. The young man paced slowly along till the sun arose, when he commenced traveling at his accustomed speed. He passed the day in running, and although he could not see any where on the horizon the Red Swan, he thought that he discerned a faint red light far over in the west.

When night came, he was pleased to find himself near another village; and when at a distance he heard the watchman crying out, "We are visited;" and soon the men of the village stood out to see the stranger.

He was again told to enter the lodge of the chief, and his reception was in every respect the same as on the previous night; except that the young woman was more beautiful, and that she entertained him very kindly. Although urged to stay with them, the mind of Maidwa was fixed on the object of his journey.

Before daybreak he asked the young woman at what time the Red Swan passed, and to point out the way. She marked against the sky with her finger the course it had taken, and told him that it had passed yesterday when the sun was between mid-day and its falling-place.

Maidwa again set out rather slowly, but when the sun had risen, he tried his speed by shooting an arrow ahead, and running after it; but it fell behind him, and he knew that he had lost nothing of his quickness of foot.

Nothing remarkable happened through the day, and he went on leisurely. Some time after dark, as he was peering around the country for a shelter, he saw a light emitted from a small low lodge. He went up to it very slyly, and, peeping through the door, he discovered an old man alone, with his head down upon his breast, warming his back before the fire.

Maidwa thought that the old man did not know that he was standing near the door; but in this he was mistaken; for, without turning his eyes to look at him, the old man said, "Walk in, my grandchild; take a seat opposite to me, and take off your things and dry them, for you must be fatigued; and I will prepare you something to eat; you shall have something very delicate."

Maidwa accepted this kind invitation, and entered the lodge. The old man then remarked, as if in mere course of conversation: "My kettle with water stands near the fire;" and immediately a small earthen pot with legs appeared by the fire. He then took one grain of corn, also one of whortleberry, and put them in the pot.

Maidwa was very hungry, and seeing the limited scale of the old man's housekeeping, he thought his chance for a supper was very slight. The old man had promised him something very delicate, and he seemed likely to keep his word. Maidwa looked on silently, and did not change his face any more than if the greatest banquet that was ever spread had been going forward.

The pot soon boiled, when the old man said in a very quiet way :

" The pot will stand at a distance from the fire."

It removed itself, and the old man added to Maidwa :

" My grandchild, feed yourself ;" handing him at the same time a dish and ladle of the same ware as the pot itself.

The young man, whose hunger was very great, helped himself to all that was in the pot. He felt ashamed to think that he had done so, but before he could speak the old man said :

" Eat, my grandchild ; eat, eat !" and soon after he again said—" Help yourself from the pot."

Maidwa was surprised, on dipping in his ladle, to see that it was full ; and although he emptied it a second time, it was still again filled and refilled till his hunger was entirely satisfied. The old man then observed, without raising his voice :

" The pot will return to its corner ;" and the pot took itself off to its accustomed place in an out-of-the-way corner of the lodge.

Maidwa observed that the old man was about to address him, and took an attitude which showed that he was prepared to listen.

" Keep on, my grandchild," said the old man ;

"you will surely gain that you seek. To tell you
more I am not permitted; but go on as you have
begun and you will not be disappointed. To-morrow you will again reach one of my fellow old men,
but the one you will see after him will tell you all,
and the manner in which you must proceed to accomplish your journey. Often has this Red Swan
passed, and those who have followed it have never
returned; but you must be firm in your resolution,
and be prepared for all that may happen."

"So will it be," answered Maidwa; and they both
laid down to sleep.

Early in the morning the old man ordered his
magic kettle to prepare breakfast, so that his guest
might eat before leaving. As Maidwa passed out, the
old man gave him a blessing with his parting advice.

Maidwa set forth in better spirits than at any
time since he had started. Night again found him
in company with an old man who entertained him
kindly, with a frisky little kettle which hurried up
to the fire before it was spoken to, bustled about
and set his supper briskly before Maidwa, and frisked
away again, without waiting for orders. The old
man also carefully directed him on his way in the
morning.

He traveled with a light heart, as he now expected to meet the one who was to give him directions how to proceed to get the Red Swan.

Toward night-fall Maidwa reached the lodge of
the third old man. Before coming to the door he
heard him saying :

" Grandchild, come in ;" and going in promptly
he felt quite at home.

The old man prepared him something to eat, acting as the other magicians had done, and his kettle
was of the same size, and looked as if it were an own
brother of the two others which had feasted him, except that this kettle, in coming and going about its
household duties, would make a passing remark, or
sing a little tune for itself.

The old man waited until Maidwa had fully satisfied his hunger, when he addressed him :

" Young man, the errand you are bound on is be-
set with trials and difficulties. Numbers have passed
with the same purpose as that which now prompts
you, but they never returned. Be careful, and if
your guardian spirits are powerful you may succeed.
This Red Swan you are following is the daughter of
a magician who has abundance of every thing, but
only this one child, whom he values more than the
sacred arrows. In former times he wore a cap of
wampum, which was attached to his scalp ; but powerful Indians, warriors of a distant chief, came and
told him that their chief's daughter was on the brink
of the grave, and that she herself requested his wam-
pum-cap, which she was confident would save her

life. 'If I can only see it,' she said, 'I will recover.
It was for this cap they had come, and after long so-
licitation the magician at length consented to part
with it, in the hope that it would restore to health
the dying maiden, although when he took it off to
hand it to the messengers it left the crown of his
head bare and bloody. Years have passed since, and
it has not healed. The coming of the warriors to
procure it for the sick maiden was a cheat, and they
are now constantly making sport of the unhappy
scalp—dancing it about from village to village—and
on every insult it receives the poor old chief to
whom it belongs groans with pain. Those who hold
it are too powerful for the magician, and many have
sacrificed themselves to recover it for him, but without success. The Red Swan has enticed many a
young man, as she has you, to enlist them to procure
the scalp, and whoever is so fortunate as to succeed,
it is understood, will receive the Red Swan as his re-
ward. In the morning you will proceed on your way,
and toward evening you will come to this magician's
lodge. You will know it by the groans which you
will hear far over the prairie as you approach. He
will ask you in. You will see no one but himself.
He will question you much as to your dreams and
the strength of your guardian spirits. If he is satisfied with your answers, he will urge you to attempt
the recovery of his scalp. He will show you the

course to take, and if you feel inclined, as I see that you do, go forward, my son, with a strong heart; persevere, and I have a presentiment that you will succeed."

Maidwa answered, " I will try."

Betimes in the morning, after having eaten from the magic kettle, which sung a sort of farewell chant on its way from the fire-place to its station in the corner, he set off on his journey.

Toward evening, Maidwa, as he crossed a prairie, heard, as had been predicted, groans from a distant lodge, which were only interrupted by a voice from a person whom he could not see, calling to him aloud :

"Come in ! come in !"

On entering the lodge, the magician heaved a great groan from the very bottom of his chest, and Maidwa saw that the crown of his head was all bare and bloody.

" Sit down, sit down," he said, "while I prepare you something to eat. You see how poor I am. I have to attend to all my own wants, with no other servant than that poor little kettle in the corner. Kettle, we will have something to eat, if you please."

" In a moment," the kettle spoke up from the corner.

" You will oblige me by making all the dispatch you can," said the magician, in a very humble tone, still addressing the kettle.

"Have patience," replied the kettle, "and I will be with you presently."

After a considerable delay, there came forward out of the corner from which it had spoken, a great heavy-browed and pot-bodied kettle, which advanced with much stateliness and solemnity of manner till it had come directly in front of the magician, whom it addressed with the question :

"What shall we have, sir ?"

"Corn, if you please," the magician answered.

"No, we will have whortleberries," rejoined the kettle, in a firm voice.

"Very well ; just as you choose."

When he supposed it was time, the magician invited Maidwa to help himself.

"Hold a minute," interposed the kettle, as Maidwa was about to dip in his ladle. He paused, and after a delay, the kettle, shaking itself up and simmering very loudly, said, "Now we are ready."

Maidwa fell to and satisfied his hunger.

"Will the kettle now withdraw ?" asked the magician, with an air of much deference.

"No," said the kettle, "we will stay and hear what the young man has to say for himself."

"Very well," said the magician. "You see," he added to Maidwa, "how poor I am. I have to take counsel with the kettle, or I should be all alone, without a day's food, and with no one to advise me."

All this time the Red Swan was carefully con-cealed in the lodge, behind a curtain, from which Maidwa heard now and then a rustling noise, that fluttered his spirits and set his heart to beating at a wonderful rate.

As soon as Maidwa had partaken of food and laid aside his leggings and moccasins, the old magician commenced telling him how he had lost his scalp, the insults it was receiving, the pain he suffered thereby, his wishes to regain it, the many unsuccess-ful attempts that had already been made, and the numbers and power of those who retained it. He would interrupt his discourse, at times, with sudden groans, and say :

" Oh, how shamefully they are treating it."

Maidwa listened to all the old magician had to say with solemn attention.

The magician renewed his discourse, and inquired of Maidwa as to his dreams, or what he saw in his sleep, at such times as he had fasted and darkened his face to procure guardian spirits.

Maidwa then told him one dream. The magician groaned.

" No, that is not it," he said.

Maidwa told him of two or three others.

The magician groaned again and again, and said, rather peevishly, " No, these are not the dreams."

" Keep cool," said the kettle, which had left the

7*

fire, and was standing in the middle of the floor, where a pleasant breeze was blowing through the lodge, and added, "Have you no more dreams of another kind?"

"Yes," said Maidwa; and he told him one.

"That will do," said the kettle. "We are much pleased with that."

"Yes, that is it—that is it!" the magician added. "You will cause me to live. That was what I was wishing you to say. Will you then go and see if you can not recover my poor scalp?"

"Yes," said Maidwa, "I will go; and the day after to-morrow, when you hear the ka-kak cries of the hawk, you will know that I am successful. You must prepare your head, and lean it out through the door, so that the moment I arrive I may place your scalp on."

"Yes, yes," said the magician. "As you say it will be done."

Early the next morning Maidwa set out to fulfill his promise; and in the afternoon, when the sun hangs toward home, he heard the shouts of a great many people. He was in a wood at the time, and saw, as he thought, only a few men, but as he went on they increased in numbers. On emerging upon the plain, their heads appeared like the hanging leaves, they were so many.

In the middle of the plain he perceived a post, and

something waving at its top. It was the wampum scalp; and every now and then the air was rent with the war-song, for they were dancing the war-dance in high spirit around it.

Before he could be observed, Maidwa changed himself into a humming-bird, and flew toward the scalp. As he passed some of those who were standing by, he came close to their ears, and as they heard the rapid whirr or murmur which this bird makes when it flies, they jumped aside, and asked each other what it could be. Maidwa had nearly reached the scalp, but fearing that he should be perceived while untying it, he again changed himself into the down that floats lightly on the air, and sailed slowly on to the scalp. He loosened it, and moved off heavily, as the weight was almost too great for him to bear up. The Indians around would have snatched it away had not a lucky current of air just then buoyed him up. As they saw that it was moving away they cried out, "It is taken from us! it is taken from us!"

Maidwa was borne gently along but a little way above their heads; and as they followed him, the rush and hum of the people was like the dead beating of the surges upon a lake shore after a storm. But the good wind gaining strength, soon carried him beyond their pursuit. A little further on he changed himself into a hawk, and flew swiftly off with his trophy, crying, "Ka-kak! ka-kak!" till it resounded with its shrill tone through the whole country, far and wide.

Meanwhile the magician had remembered the intructions of Maidwa, placing his head outside of the lodge as soon as he heard the ka-kak cry of the hawk

In a moment Maidwa came past with rustling wings, and as he flew by, giving the magician a severe blow on the head with the wampum scalp, his limbs extended and quivered in an agony, the scalp adhered, and Maidwa, in his own person, walked into the lodge and sat down, feeling perfectly at home.

The magician was so long in recovering from the stunning blow which had been dealt him, that Maidwa feared that in restoring the crown of his head he had destroyed his life. Presently, however, he was pleased to see him show, by the motion of his hands and limbs, that his strength was returning; and in a little while he rose and stood upon his feet. What was the delight of Maidwa to behold, instead of a withered old man, far advanced in years and stricken in sorrow, a bright and cheerful youth, who glittered with life as he stood up before him.

"Thank you, my friend," he said. "Your kindness and bravery of heart have restored me to my former shape. It was so ordained, and you have now accomplished the victory."

They embraced; and the young magician urged the stay of his deliverer for a few days, and they formed a strong attachment to each other. The magician, to the deep regret of Maidwa, never once alluded to the Red Swan in all their conferences.

At last the day arrived when Maidwa prepared to return to his home. The young magician bestowed on him ample presents of wampum, fur, robes, and other costly things. Although Maidwa's heart was burning within him to see the Red Swan, to hear her spoken of, and to learn what his fortune was to be in regard to that fond object of his pursuit, he constrained his feelings, and so checked his countenance as to never look where he supposed she might be. His friend the young magician observed the same silence and caution.

Maidwa's pack for traveling was now ready, and he was taking his farewell smoke, when the young magician thus addressed him: " My friend Maidwa, you know for what cause you came thus far, and why you have risked so much and waited so long. You have proved my friend indeed. You have accomplished your object, and your noble perseverance shall not go unrewarded. If you undertake other things with the same spirit, you will always succeed. My destiny compels me to remain where I am, although I should feel happy to be allowed to go with you. I have given you, of ordinary gifts, all you will need as long as you live; but I see you are backward to speak of the Red Swan. I vowed that whoever procured me my lost wampum-scalp should be rewarded by possessing the Red Swan."

He then spoke in a language which Maidwa did not understand, the curtain of the lodge parted, and the Red Swan met his gaze. It was a beautiful female that he beheld, so majestical and airy in her look, that he seemed to see a creature whose home should rather be in the free heaven, and among the rosy clouds, than in this dusky lodge.

"Take her," the young magician said; "she is my sister; treat her well. She is worthy of you, and what you have done for me merits more. She is ready to go with you to your kindred and friends, and has been so ever since your arrival; and my good wishes shall go with you both."

The Red Swan smiled kindly on Maidwa, who advanced and greeted her. Hand in hand they took their way forth from the lodge, and, watched by the young magician, advanced across the prairie on their homeward course.

They traveled slowly, and looked with double joy on the beautiful country over which they had both so lately passed with hearts ill at ease.

After two or three days they reached the lodge of the third old man who had entertained him with the singing kettle; but the kettle was not there. The old man, nevertheless, received them very kindly, and said to Maidwa, "You see what your perseverance has secured you; do so always, and you will succeed in whatever you undertake."

On the following morning, when they were about to start, he pulled from the side of the lodge a bag, which he presented to Maidwa, saying, "Grandchild, I give you this; it contains a present for you; and I hope you will live happily till old age."

Bidding him farewell, they again set forward; and they soon came to the second old man's lodge; he also gave them a present and bestowed his blessing. Nor did Maidwa see any thing here of the frisky little kettle which had been so lively on his former visit.

As they went on and came to the lodge of the first old man, their reception and farewell were the same; and when Maidwa glanced to the corner, the silent kettle, which had been the first acquaintance he had made in that family on his travels, was not there. The old man smiled when he discovered the direction of Maidwa's glance, but he said nothing.

When, on continuing their journey, they at last approached the first town which Maidwa had passed in his pursuit, the watchman gave notice as before, and he was shown into the chief's lodge.

"Sit down there, son-in-law," said the chief, pointing to a place near his daughter. "And you also," he said to the Red Swan.

The chief's daughter was engaged in coloring a girdle, and, as if indifferent to these visitors, she did not even raise her head. Presently the chief said, " Let some one bring in the bundle of our son-in-law."

When the bundle was laid before him, Maidwa opened one of the bags which had been given to him. It was filled with various costly articles—wampum, robes, and trinkets, of much richness and value; these, in token of his kindness, he presented to the chief. The chief's daughter stole a glance at the costly gifts, then at Maidwa and his beautiful wife. She stopped working, and was silent and thoughtful all the evening. The chief himself talked with Maidwa of his adventures, congratulated him on his good fortune, and concluded by telling him that he should take his daughter along with him in the morning.

Maidwa said " Yes."

The chief then spoke up, saying, " Daughter, be ready to go with him in the morning."

Now it happened when the chief was thus speaking that there was a foolish fellow in the lodge, who had thought to have got this chief's daughter for a wife ; and he jumped up, saying :

" Who is he," looking grimly at Maidwa, " that he should take her for a few presents ?   I will kill him."

And he raised a knife which he had in his hand, and gave it a mighty flourish in the air. He kept up this terrible flourish till some one came and

pulled him back to his seat, which he had been waiting for, and then he sat quiet enough.

Amid the greetings of their new friends, Maidwa
and the Red Swan, with the chief's daughter, took
their leave by peep of day, and toward evening they
reached the other town. The watchman gave the
signal, and numbers of men, women and children
stood out to see them. They were again shown into
the chief's lodge, who welcomed him, saying :

" Son-in-law, you are welcome."

And he requested Maidwa to take a seat by his
daughter, and the two women did the same.

After suitable refreshment for all, and while Maidwa smoked a pipe, the chief asked him to relate his
adventures in the hearing of all the inmates of the
lodge, and of the strangers who had gathered in at
report of his singular fortunes.

Maidwa gave them his whole story. When he
came to those parts which related to the Red Swan,
they turned and looked upon her in wonder and admiration, for she was very beautiful.

The chief then informed Maidwa that his brothers
had been to their town in search of him, but that
they had gone back some time before, having given
up all hopes of ever seeing him again. He added,
that since he had shown himself a man of spirit,
whom fortune was pleased to befriend, he should take
his daughter with him.

" For although your brothers," he said, " were here, they were too bashful to enter any of our lodges. They merely inquired for you and returned. You will take my daughter, treat her well, and that will bind us more closely together."

It is always the case in an assembly or gathering that some one of the number is foolish, and disposed to play the clown. It happened to be so here. One of this very sort was in the lodge, and, after Maidwa had given the old chief presents, as he had to the other, this pretender jumped up in a passion, and cried out :

" Who is this stranger, that he should have her ? I want her myself."

The chief bade him be quiet, and not to disturb or quarrel with one who was enjoying their hospitality.

" No, no," he exclaimed, rushing forward as in act to strike.

Maidwa sat unmoved, and paid no heed to his threats.

He cried the louder—" I will have her, I will have her !" whereupon the old chief, being now vexed past patience, took his great war-club and tapped this clownish fellow upon the head, which so far subdued him that he sat for some time quite still; when, after a while, he came to himself, the chief upbraided him for his folly, and told him to go out and tell stories to the old women.

When at last Maidwa was about to leave, he invited a number of the families of the chief to go with him and visit their hunting-grounds, where he promised them that they would find game in abundance. They consented, and in the morning a large company assembled and joined Maidwa; and the chief, with a party of warriors, escorted them a long distance. When ready to return, the chief made a speech and besought the blessing of the Good Spirit on Maidwa and his friends.

They parted, each on its course, making music with their war-drums, which could be heard from afar as they glittered with waving feathers in the morning sun, in their march over the prairie, which was lost in the distant sky.

After several days' travel, Maidwa and his friends came in sight of his home. The others rested within the woods while he went alone in advance to see his brothers.

He entered the lodge. It was all in confusion and covered with ashes. On one side, sitting among the cinders, with his face blackened, and crying aloud, was his elder brother. On the other side sat the younger, Jeekewis, also with blackened face, his head covered with stray feathers and tufts of swan-down. This one presented so curious a figure that Maidwa could not keep from laughing. He seemed to be so lost and far-gone in grief that he could not notice his brother's arrival. The eldest, however, after a while, lifting up his head, recognized Maidwa, jumped up and shook hands, and kissed him, and expressed much joy at his return.

Maidwa, as soon as he had seen the lodge set in order, made known that he had brought each of them a wife. As soon as Jeekewis heard a wife spoken of, he roused from his torpor, sprang to his feet, and said :

" Why is it just now that you have come ?" and at once made for the door and peeped out to see the strangers. He then commenced jumping and laughing, and crying out, " Women ! women !" and that was all the reception he gave his brother. Maidwa told them to wash themselves and prepare, for he would go and fetch the females in.

Jeekewis scampered about, and began to wash himself ; but he would every now and then, with one side of his head all feathers, and the other clear and shining, peep forth to look at the women again. When they came near, he said, " I will have this and that one ;" he did not exactly know which ; he would sit down for an instant, and then rise, and peep about and laugh ; in fact he acted like one beside himself.

As soon as order was restored, and all the company who had been brought in were seated, Maidwa presented one of the chief's daughters to his eldest brother, saying: " These women were given to me, to dispose of in marriage. I now give one to each. I intended so from the first."

Jeekewis spoke up and said, "I think three wives would have been enough for you."

Maidwa led the other daughter to Jeekewis, and said, "My brother, here is one for you, and live happily."

Jeekewis hung down his head as if he was ashamed, but he would every now and then steal a look at his wife and also at the other women.

By and by he turned toward his wife and acted as if he had been married for years.

Maidwa seeing that no preparation had been made to entertain the company, said, "Are we to have no supper?"

He had no sooner spoken, than forth from a corner stepped the silent kettle, which placed itself by the fire, and began bubbling and boiling quite briskly. Presently that was joined by the big talking kettle, which said, addressing itself to Maidwa, "Master, we shall be ready presently;" and then, dancing along, came, from still another, the frisky little kettle, which hopped to their side, and took an active part in the preparations for the evening meal. When all was nearly ready, a delicate voice was heard singing in the last corner of the lodge, and keeping up its dainty carol all the way to the fire-place, the fourth kettle joined the three cooks, and they all fell to with all their might, and in the best possible humor, to dispatch their work.

It was not long before the big kettle advanced toward Maidwa, and said, in his own confident way, "Supper is ready!"

The feast was a jovial one; and although they were all hungry, and plied their ladles with right good will, yet, dip in as often as they would, the four magic kettles held out, and had plenty to the end of the revel.

To draw to a close, Maidwa and his friends lived in peace for a time; their town prospered; there was no lack of children ; and every thing else was in abundance.

One day the two brothers began to look dark upon Maidwa, and to reproach him for having taken from the medicine-sack their deceased father's magic arrows; they upbraided him especially that one was lost.

After listening to them in silence, he said that he would go in search of it, and that it should be restored; and the very next day, true to his word, he left them.

After traveling a long way, and looking in every direction, almost hopeless of discovering the lost treasure, he came to an opening in the earth, and descending, it led him to the abode of departed spirits. The country appeared beautiful, the pastures were greener than his own, and the sky bluer than that which hung over the lodge, and the extent of it was utterly lost in a dim distance; and he saw animals of every kind wandering about in great numbers. The first he came to were buffalos; his surprise was great when they addressed him as human beings.

They asked him what he came for, how he had descended, and why he was so bold as to visit the abode of the dead.

He answered that he was in quest of a magic arrow, to appease the anger of his brothers.

"Very well," said the leader of the buffalos, whose form was nothing but bone. "Yes, we know it," and he and his followers moved off a little space from Maidwa, as if they were afraid of him. "You have come," resumed the buffalo-spirit, "to a place where a living man has never before been. You will return immediately to your tribe, for, under pretense of recovering one of the magic arrows which belong to you by your father's dying wish, they have sent you off that they might become possessed of your beautiful wife, the Red Swan. Speed home! You will find the magic arrow at the lodge-door. You will live to a very old age, and die happily. You can go no further in these abodes of ours."

Maidwa looked, as he thought, to the west, and saw a bright light as if the sun was shining in its splendor, but he saw no sun.

"What light is that yonder?" he asked.

The all-boned buffalo answered—"It is the place where those who were good dwell."

"And that dark cloud?" Maidwa again asked.

"It is the place of the wicked," answered the buffalo.

Maidwa turned away, for it was very dark, and it pained his eyes to look upon it; and, moving away by the aid of his guardian spirits, he again stood upon the earth, and beheld the sun giving light as usual.

All else that he learned in the abodes of the dead, and his travels and acts previous to his return homeward, are unknown, for he never spoke of them to any human being.

After wandering a long time to gather knowledge to make his people happy and to add to their comfort, he one evening drew near to his own village. Passing all the other lodges he came to his own door, where he found the magic arrow, as he had been promised. He heard his brothers from within at high words with each other. They were quarreling for the possession of his wife, who, through all his absence, had remained constant, and sadly awaited his return. Maidwa listened in shame and sorrow.

He entered the lodge, holding his head aloft as one conscious of good principle and shining with anger. He spoke not a word, but, placing the magic arrow

to his bow, he would have laid his brothers dead at
his feet ; but just then the talking kettle stepped forward and spoke such words of wisdom, and the singing kettle trolled forth such a soothing little song,
and the guilty brothers were so contrite and keenly
repentant of their intended wrong, and the Red
Swan was so radiant and forgiving, the silent kettle
straightway served them up so hearty and wholesome
a meal, and the frisky little kettle was so joyful and
danced about so merrily, that when the magic arrows
were laid away in the medicine-sack by Maidwa,
there was that night in all the Indian country no
happier family than the three brothers, who ever
after dwelt together in all kindness, as all good
brothers should.

8

XIV.

THE MAN WITH HIS LEG TIED UP.

As a punishment for having once upon a time used that foot against a venerable medicine man, Aggo Dah Gauda had one leg looped up to his thigh, so that he was obliged to get along by hopping. By dint of practice he had become very skillful in this exercise, and he could make leaps which seemed almost incredible.

Aggo had a beautiful daughter, and his chief care was to secure her from being carried off by the king of the buffalos, who was the ruler of all the herds of that kind, and had them entirely at his command to make them do as he willed.

Dah Gauda, too, was quite an important person in his own way, for he lived in great state, having a log house of his own, and a court-yard which extended from the sill of his front-door as many hundred miles westward as he chose to measure it.

Although he might claim this extensive privilege of ground, he advised his daughter to keep within doors, and by no means to go far in the neighborhood,

THE MAN WITH HIS LEG TIED UP. Page 178.

as she would otherwise be sure to be stolen away, as he was satisfied that the buffalo-king spent night and day lurking about and lying in wait to seize her.

One sunshiny morning, when there were just two or three promising clouds rolling moistly about the sky, Aggo prepared to go out a-fishing ; but before he left the lodge he reminded her of her strange and industrious lover, whom she had never seen.

" My daughter," said he, " I am going out to fish, and as the day will be a pleasant one, you must recollect that we have an enemy near, who is constantly going about with two eyes that never close, and do not expose yourself out of the lodge."

With this excellent advice, Aggo hopped off in high spirits ; but he had scarcely reached the fishing-ground when he heard a voice singing, at a distance:

> Man with the leg tied up,
> Man with the leg tied up,
> Broken hip—hip—
> Hipped.

> Man with the leg tied up,
> Man with the leg tied up,
> Broken leg—leg—
> Legged.

There was no one in sight, but Aggo heard the words quite plainly, and as he suspected the ditty to be the work of his enemies, the buffalos, he hopped home as fast as his one leg could carry him.

Meantime, the daughter had no sooner been left alone in the lodge than she thought with herself:

"It is hard to be thus forever kept in doors. But my father says it would be dangerous to venture abroad. I know what I will do. I will get on the top of the house, and there I can comb and dress my hair, and no one can harm me."

She accordingly ascended the roof and busied herself in untying and combing her beautiful hair; for it was truly beautiful, not only of a fine, glossy quality, but it was so very long that it hung over the eaves of the house and reached down on the ground, as she sat dressing it.

She was wholly occupied in this employment, without a thought of danger, when, all of a sudden, the king of the buffalos came dashing on with his herd of followers, and making sure of her by means of her drooping tresses, he placed her upon the back of one of his favorite buffalos, and away he cantered over the plains. Plunging into a river that bounded his land, he bore her safely to his lodge on the other side.

And now the buffalo-king having secured the beau-tiful person of Aggo Dah Gauda's daughter, he set to work to make her heart his own—a little ceremony which it would have been, perhaps, wiser for his majesty, the king of the buffalos, to have attended to before, for he now worked to little purpose. Although he labored with great zeal to gain her affections, she sat pensive and disconsolate in the lodge, among the other females, and scarcely ever spoke, nor did she take the least interest in the affairs of the king's household.

To the king himself she paid no heed, and although he breathed forth to her every soft and gentle word he could think of, she sat still and motionless for all the world like one of the lowly bushes by the door of her father's lodge, when the summer wind has died away.

The king enjoined it upon the others in the lodge as a special edict, on pain of instant death, to give to Aggo's daughter every thing that she wanted, and to be careful not to displease her. They set before her the choicest food. They gave her the seat of honor in the lodge. The king himself went out hunting to obtain the most dainty meats, both of animals and wild fowl, to pleasure her palate; and he treated her every morning to a ride upon one of the royal buffalos, who was so gentle in his motions as not even to disturb a single one of the tresses of the beautiful hair of Aggo's daughter as she paced along.

And not content with these proofs of his attachment, the king would sometimes fast from all food, and having thus purified his spirit and cleared his voice, he would take his Indian flute, and, sitting before the lodge, give vent to his feelings in pensive echoes, something after this fashion :

My sweetheart,
My sweetheart,
　　Ah me !
When I think of you,
When I think of you,
　　Ah me !
What can I do, do, do?

How I love you,
How I love you,
　　Ah me !
Do not hate me,
Do not hate me,
　　Ah me !
Speak—e'en berate me.
When I think of you,
　　Ah me !
What can I do, do, do ?

In the mean time, Aggo Dah Gauda had reached home, and finding that his daughter had been stolen, his indignation was so thoroughly awakened that he would have forthwith torn every hair from his head, but, being entirely bald, this was out of the question, so, as an easy and natural vent to his feelings, Aggo hopped off half a mile in every direction. First he hopped east, then he hopped west, next he hopped north, and again he hopped south, all in search of his daughter; till the one leg was fairly tired out. Then he sat down in his lodge, and resting himself a little, he reflected, and then he vowed that his single leg should never know rest again until he had found his beautiful daughter and brought her home. For this purpose he immediately set out.

Now that he proceeded more coolly, he could easily track the buffalo-king until he came to the banks of the river, where he saw that he had plunged in and swam over. There having been a frosty night or two since, the water was so covered with thin ice that Aggo could not venture upon it, even with one leg. He encamped hard by till it became more solid, and then crossed over and pursued the trail.

As he went along he saw branches broken off and strewed behind, which guided him in his course; for these had been purposely cast along by the daughter. And the manner in which she had accomplished it was this. Her hair was all untied when she was caught up, and being very long it took hold of the branches as they darted along, and it was these twigs that she broke off as signs to her father.

When Aggo came to the king's lodge it was evening. Carefully approaching, he peeped through the sides, and saw his daughter sitting disconsolate. She immediately caught his eye, and knowing that it was her father come for her, she all at once appeared to relent in her heart, and, asking for the royal dipper, said to the king, "I will go and get you a drink of water."

This token of submission delighted his majesty,

and, high in hope, he waited with impatience for her return.

At last he went out, but nothing could be seen or heard of the captive daughter. Calling together his followers, they sallied forth upon the plains, and had not gone far when they espied by the light of the moon, which was shining roundly just over the edge of the prairie, Aggo Dah Gauda, his daughter in his arms, making all speed with his one leg toward the west.

The buffalos being set on by their king, raised a great shout, and scampered off in pursuit. They thought to overtake Aggo in less than no time; but although he had a single leg only, it was in such fine condition to go, that to every pace of theirs, he hopped the length of a cedar-tree.

But the buffalo-king was well assured that he would be able to overtake Aggo, hop as briskly as he might. It would be a mortal shame, thought the king, to be outstripped by a man with one leg tied up; so, shouting and cheering, and issuing orders on all sides, he set the swiftest of his herd upon the track, with strict commands to take Aggo dead or alive. And a curious sight it was to see.

At one time a buffalo would gain handsomely upon Aggo, and be just at the point of laying hold of him, when off Aggo would hop, a good furlong, in an oblique line, wide out of his reach; which bringing him nearly in contact with another of the herd, away he would go again, just as far off in another direction.

And in this way Aggo kept the whole company of the buffalos zig-zagging across the plain, with the poor king at their head, running to and fro, shouting among them and hurrying them about in the wildest way. It was an extraordinary road that Aggo was taking toward home; and after a time it so puzzled and bewildered the buffalos that they were driven half out of their wits, and they roared, and brandished their tails, and foamed, as if they would put out of countenance and frighten out of sight the old man in the moon, who was looking on all the time, just above the edge of the prairie.

As for the king himself, losing at last all patience at the absurd idea of chasing a man with one leg all night long, he called his herd together, and fled, in disgust, toward the west, and never more appeared in all that part of the country.

Aggo, relieved of his pursuers, hopped off a hundred steps in one, till he reached the stream, crossed it in a twinkling of the eye, and bore his daughter in triumph to his lodge.

In the course of time Aggo's beautiful daughter married a very worthy young warrior, who was neither a buffalo-king nor so much as the owner of any more

of the buffalos than a splendid skin robe which he
wore, with great effect, thrown over his shoulders, on
his wedding-day.   On which occasion, Aggo Dah
Gauda hopped about on his one leg livelier than
ever.

XV.

THE LITTLE SPIRIT, OR BOY-MAN.

IN a little lodge at a beautiful spot on a lake shore, alone with his sister, lived a boy remarkable for the smallness of his stature. Many large rocks were scattered around their habitation, and it had a very wild and out-of-the-way look.

The boy grew no larger as he advanced in years, and yet, small as he was, he had a big spirit of his own, and loved dearly to play the master in the lodge. One day in winter he told his sister to make him a ball to play with, as he meant to have some sport along the shore on the clear ice. When she handed him the ball, his sister cautioned him not to go too far.

He laughed at her, and posted off in high glee, throwing his ball before him and running after it at full speed, and he went as fast as his ball. At last his ball flew to a great distance ; he followed as fast as he could. After he had run forward for some time, he saw what seemed four dark spots upon the ice, straight before him.

When he came up to the shore he was surprised to see four large, tall men, lying on the ice, spearing fish. They were four brothers, who looked exactly alike. As the little boy-man approached them, the nearest looked up, and in his turn he was surprised to see such a tiny being, and turning to his brothers, he said :

"Tia ! look ! see what a little fellow is here."

The three others thereupon looked up too, and seeing these four faces, as if they had been one, the little spirit or boy-man said to himself :

"Four in one ! What a time they must have in choosing their hunting-shirts !"

After they had all stared for a moment at the boy, they covered their heads, intent in searching for fish. The boy thought to himself :

"These four-faces fancy that I am to be put off without notice because I am so little, and they are so broad and long. They shall find out. I may find a way to teach them that I am not to be treated so lightly."

After they were covered up, the boy-man, looking sharply about, saw that among them they had caught one large trout, which was lying just by their side. Stealing along, he slyly seized it, and placing his fingers in the gills, and tossing his ball before him, he ran off at full speed.

They heard the pattering of his little steps upon

the ice, and when the four looked up all together, they saw their fine trout sliding away, as if of itself, at a great rate, the boy being so small that he could not be distinguished from the fish.

"See !" they cried out, "our fish is running away on the dry land !"

When they stood up they could just see, over the fish's head, that it was the boy-man who was carrying it off.

The little spirit reached the lodge, and having left the trout at the door, he told his sister to go out and bring in the fish he had brought home.

She exclaimed, "Where could you have got it ? I hope you have not stolen it."

"Oh," he replied, "I found it on the ice. It was caught in our lake. Have we no right to a little lake of our own ? I shall claim all the fish that come out of its waters."

"How," the sister asked again, "could you have got it there ?"

"No matter," said the boy ; "go and cook it.'

It was as much as the girl could do to drag the great trout within doors. She cooked it, and its flavor was so delicious that she asked no more questions as to how he had come by it.

The next morning the little spirit or boy-man set off as he had the day before.

He made all sorts of sport with his ball as he frol-

icked along—high over his head he would toss it,
straight up into the air; then far before him, and
again, in mere merriment of spirit, he would send it
bounding back, as if he had plenty of speed and
enough to spare in running back after it. And the
ball leaped and bounded about, and glided through
the air as if it were a live thing, and enjoyed the
sport as much as the boy-man himself.

When he came within hail of the four large men,
who were fishing there every day, he cast his ball
with such force that it rolled into the ice-hole about
which they were busy. The boy, standing on the
shore of the lake, called out:

" Four-in-one, pray hand me my ball."

" No, indeed," they answered, setting up a grim
laugh which curdled their four dark faces all at once,
" we shall not ;" and with their fishing-spears they
thrust the ball under the ice.

" Good !" said the boy-man, " we shall see."

Saying which he rushed upon the four brothers and
thrust them at one push into the water. His ball
bounded back to the surface, and, picking it up, he
ran off, tossing it before him in his own sportive way.
Outstripping it in speed he soon reached home, and
remained within till the next morning.

The four brothers, rising up from the water at the
same time, dripping and wroth, roared out in one
voice a terrible threat of vengeance, which they prom-

ised to execute the next day. They knew the boy's speed, and that they could by no means overtake him.

By times in the morning, the four brothers were stirring in their lodge, and getting ready to look after their revenge.

Their old mother, who lived with them, begged them not to go.

" Better," said she, " now that your clothes are dry, to think no more of the ducking than to go and all four of you get your heads broken, as you surely will, for that boy is a monedo or he could not perform such feats as he does."

But her sons paid no heed to this wise advice, and, raising a great war-cry, which frightened the birds overhead nearly out of their feathers, they started for the boy's lodge among the rocks.

The little spirit or boy-man heard them roaring forth their threats as they approached, but he did not appear to be disquieted in the least. His sister as yet had heard nothing ; after a while she thought she could distinguish the noise of snow-shoes on the snow, at a distance, but rapidly advancing. She looked out, and seeing the four large men coming straight to their lodge she was in great fear, and running in, exclaimed :

" He is coming, four times as strong as ever !" for she supposed that the one man whom her brother had offended had become so angry as to make four of himself in order to wreak his vengeance.

The boy-man said, "Why do you mind them? Give me something to eat."

"How can you think of eating at such a time?" she replied.

"Do as I request you, and be quick."

She then gave little spirit his dish, and he commenced eating.

Just then the brothers came to the door.

"See!" cried the sister, "the man with four heads!"

The brothers were about to lift the curtain at the door, when the boy-man turned his dish upside down, and immediately the door was closed with a stone; upon which the four brothers set to work and hammered with their clubs with great fury, until at length they succeeded in making a slight opening. One of the brothers presented his face at this little window, and rolled his eye about at the boy-man in a very threatening way.

The little spirit, who, when he had closed the door, had returned to his meal, which he was quietly eating, took up his bow and arrow which lay by his side, and let fly the shaft, which, striking the man in the head, he fell back. The boy-man merely called out "Number one" as he fell, and went on with his meal. In a moment a second face, just like the first, presented itself; and as he raised his bow, his sister said to him:

"What is the use? You have killed that man already."

Little spirit fired his arrow—the man fell—he called out "Number two," and continued his meal.

The two others of the four brothers were dispatched in the same quiet way, and counted off as "Number three" and "Number four."

After they were all well disposed of in this way, the boy-man directed his sister to go out and see them. She presently ran back, saying:

"There are four of them."

"Of course," the boy-man answered, "and there always shall be four of them."

Going out himself, the boy-man raised the brothers to their feet, and giving each a push, one with his face to the East, another to the West, a third to the South, and the last to the North, he sent them off to wander about the earth; and whenever you see four men just alike, they are the four brothers whom the little spirit or boy-man dispatched upon their travels.

But this was not the last display of the boy-man's power.

When spring came on, and the lake began to sparkle in the morning sun, the boy-man said to his sister:

"Make me a new set of arrows, and a bow."

Although he provided for their support, the little spirit never performed household or hard work of any kind, and his sister obeyed.

When she had made the weapons, which, though they were very small, were beautifully wrought and of the best stuff the field and wood could furnish, she again cautioned him not to shoot into the lake.

"She thinks," said the boy-man to himself, "I can see no further into the water than she. My sister shall learn better."

Regardless of her warnings, he on purpose discharged a shaft into the lake, waded out into the water till he got into its depth, and paddled about for his arrow, so as to call the attention of his sister, and as if to show that he hardily braved her advice.

She hurried to the shore, calling on him to return; but instead of heeding her, he cried out:

"You of the red fins, come and swallow me!"

Although his sister did not clearly understand whom her brother was addressing, she too called out:

"Don't mind the foolish boy!"

The boy-man's order seemed to be best attended to, for immediately a monstrous fish came and swallowed him. Before disappearing entirely, catching a glimpse of his sister standing in despair upon the shore, the boy-man hallooed out to her:

"Me-zush-ke-zin-ance!"

She wondered what he meant. At last it occurred to her that it must be an old moccasin. She accordingly ran to the lodge, and bringing one, she tied it to a string attached to a tree, and cast it into the water

The great fish said to the boy-man under water :

" What is that floating ?"

To which the boy-man replied :

" Go, take hold of it, swallow it as fast as you can ' it is a great delicacy."

The fish darted toward the old shoe and swallowed it, making of it a mere mouthful.

The boy-man laughed in himself, but said nothing, till the fish was fairly caught, when he took hold of the line and began to pull himself in his fish-carriage ashore.

The sister, who was watching all this time, opened wide her eyes as the huge fish came up and up upon the shore; and she opened them still more when the fish seemed to speak, and she heard from within a voice, saying, " Make haste and release me from this nasty place."

It was her brother's voice, which she was accustomed to obey; and she made haste with her knife to open a door in the side of the fish, from which the boy-man presently leaped forth. He lost no time in ordering her to cut it up and dry it; telling her that their spring supply of meat was now provided.

The sister now began to believe that her brother

was an extraordinary boy; yet she was not altogether satisfied in her mind that he was greater than the rest of the world.

They sat, one evening, in the lodge, musing with each other in the dark, by the light of each other's eyes—for they had no other of any kind—when the sister said, "My brother, it is strange that you, who can do so much, are no wiser than the Ko-ko, who gets all his light from the moon; which shines or not, as it pleases."

"And is not that light enough?" asked the little spirit.

"Quite enough," the sister replied. "If it would but come within the lodge and not sojourn out in the tree-tops and among the clouds."

"We will have a light of our own, sister," said the boy-man; and, casting himself upon a mat by the door, he commenced singing:

> Fire-fly, fire-fly, bright little thing,
> Light me to bed and my song I will sing;
> Give me your light, as you fly o'er my head,
> That I may merrily go to my bed.
>
> Give me your light o'er the grass as you creep,
> That I may joyfully go to my sleep;
> Come, little fire-fly, come little beast,
> Come! and I'll make you to-morrow a feast.
>
> Come, little candle, that flies as I sing,
> Bright little fairy-bug, night's little king;
> Come and I'll dream as you guide me along;
> Come and I'll pay you, my bug, with a song.

As the boy-man chanted this call, they came in at first one by one, then in couples, till at last, swarming in little armies, the fire-flies lit up the little lodge with a thousand sparkling lamps, just as the stars were lighting the mighty hollow of the sky without.

The faces of the sister and brother shone upon each other, from their opposite sides of the lodge, with a kindly gleam of mutual trustfulness; and never more from that hour did a doubt of each other darken their little household.

XVI.

THE ENCHANTED MOCCASINS.

A LONG, long time ago, a little boy was living with his sister entirely alone in an uninhabited country, far out in the north-west. He was called the Boy that carries the Ball on his Back, from an idea that he possessed supernatural powers. This boy was in the habit of meditating alone, and asking within himself, whether there were other beings similar to themselves on the earth.

When he grew up to manhood, he inquired of his sister whether she knew of any human beings beside themselves. She replied that she did; and that there was, at a great distance, a large village.

As soon as he heard this, he said to his sister, " I am now a young man and very much in want of a companion;" and he asked his sister to make him several pairs of moccasins.

She complied with his request; and as soon as he received the moccasins, he took up his war-club and set out in quest of the distant village.

He traveled on till he came to a small wigwam, and on looking into it he discovered a very old woman sitting alone by the fire. As soon as she saw the stranger, she invited him in, and thus addressed him:

"My poor grandchild, I suppose you are one of those who seek for the distant village, from which no person has ever yet returned. Unless your guardian is more powerful than the guardians of those who have gone before you, you will share a similar fate to theirs. Be careful to provide yourself with the invisible bones they use in the medicine-dance, for without these you can not succeed.'

After she had thus spoken, she gave him the following directions for his journey:

"When you come near to the village which you seek, you will see in the center a large lodge, in which the chief of the village, who has two daughters, resides. Before the door there is a great tree, which is smooth and without bark. On this tree, about the height of a man from the ground, is hung a small lodge, in which these two false daughters dwell. It is here that so many have been destroyed, and among them your two elder brothers. Be wise, my grandchild, and abide strictly by my directions."

The old woman then gave to the young man the bones which were to secure his success; and she informed him with great care how he was to proceed.

Placing them in his bosom, Onwee Bahmondang, or the Wearer of the Ball, continued his journey, and kept eagerly on until he arrived at the village of which he was in search; and as he was gazing around him, he saw both the tree and the lodge which the old woman had mentioned.

He at once bent his steps for the tree, and approaching, he endeavored to reach the suspended lodge. But all his efforts were in vain; for as often as he attempted to reach it, the tree began to tremble, and it soon shot up so that the lodge could hardly be perceived.

He bethought him of his guardian, and invoking his aid, and changing himself into a squirrel, he mounted nimbly up again, in the hope that the lodge would not now escape him. Away shot the lodge, climb as briskly as he might.

Panting, and out of breath, he remembered the instructions of the old woman, and drawing from his bosom one of the bones, he thrust it into the trunk of the tree, and rested himself to be ready to start again.

As often as he wearied of climbing, for even a squirrel can not climb forever, he repeated the little ceremony of the bones; but whenever he came near the lodge and put forth his hand to touch it, the tree would shoot up as before, and carry the lodge up far beyond his reach.

At length the bones being all gone, and the lodge well-nigh out of sight, he began to despair, for the earth, too, had long since vanished entirely from his view.

Summoning his whole heart, he resolved to try once more. On and up he went, and, as soon as he put forth his hand to touch it, the tree again shook, and away went the lodge.

One more endeavor, brave Onwee, and in he goes; for having now reached the arch of heaven, the fly-away lodge could go no higher.

Onwee entered the lodge with a fearless step, and he beheld the two wicked sisters sitting opposite each other. He asked their names. The one on his left hand called herself Azhabee, and the one on the right, Negahnabee.

After talking with them a little while, he discovered that whenever he addressed the one on his left hand, the tree would tremble as before and settle down to its former place; but when he addressed the one on his right hand, it would again shoot upward.

When he thus perceived that by addressing the one on his left hand that the tree would descend, he continued to do so until it had again settled down to its place near the earth. Then seizing his war-club, he said to the sisters:

" You who have caused the death of so many of

9

my brethren I will now put an end to, and thus have revenge for those you have destroyed."

As he spoke this he raised the club, and with one blow laid the two wicked women dead at his feet.

Onwee then descended, and learning that these sisters had a brother living with their father, who had shared all together in the spoils of all such as the wicked sisters had betrayed, and who would now pursue him for having put an end to their wicked profits, Onwee set off at random, not knowing whither he went.

The father coming in the evening to visit the lodge of his daughters, discovered what had happened. He immediately sent word to his son that his sisters had been slain, and that there were no more spoils to be had, which greatly inflamed the young man's temper, especially the woeful announcement at the close.

" The person who has done this," said the brother, as soon as he had reached the spot, chafing and half beside himself at the gloomy prospect of having no more travelers to strip, " must be that boy who carries the ball on his back. I know his mode of going about his business, and since he would not allow himself to be killed by my sisters, he shall have the honor of dying by my hand. I will pursue him and have revenge."

" It is well, my son," replied the father; " the

spirit of your life grant you success. I counsel you to be wary in the pursuit. Bahmondang is a cunning youth. It is a strong spirit who has put him on to do this injury to us, and he will try to deceive you in every way. Above all, avoid tasting food till you succeed ; for if you break your fast before you see his blood, your power will be destroyed."

The son took this fatherly advice all in good part, except that portion which enjoined upon him to abstain from staying his stomach ; but over that he made a number of wry faces, for the brother of the two wicked sisters had, among numerous noble gifts, a very noble appetite. Nevertheless, he took up his weapons and departed in pursuit of Onwee Bahmondang, at the top of his speed.

Onwee finding that he was closely followed, climbed up into one of the tallest trees, and shot forth the magic arrows with which he had provided himself.

Seeing that his pursuer was not turned back by his arrows, Onwee renewed his flight ; and when he found himself hard pressed, and his enemy close behind him, he transformed himself into the skeleton of a moose that had been killed, whose flesh had come off from his bones. He then remembered the moccasins which his sister had given him, and which were enchanted. Taking a pair of them, he placed them near the skeleton.

" Go," said he to them, " to the end of the earth."

The moccasins then left him, and their tracks remained.

The angry brother at length came to the skeleton of the moose, when he perceived that the track he had been long pursuing did not stop there, so he continued to follow it up till he arrived at the end of the earth, where, for all his trouble, he found only a pair of moccasins.

Vexed that he had been outwitted by following a pair of moccasins instead of their owner, who was the object of his pursuit, he bitterly complained, resolving not to give up his revenge, and to be more wary in scrutinizing signs.

He then called to mind the skeleton he had met with on his way, and concluded that it must be the object of his search.

He retraced his steps toward the skeleton, but to his surprise it had disappeared, and the tracks of the wearer of the ball were in another direction. He now became faint with hunger, and lost heart ; but when he remembered the blood of his sisters, and that he should not be allowed to enjoy a meal, nor so much as a mouthful, until he had put an end to Onwee Bahmondang, he plucked up his spirits and determined again to pursue.

Onwee, finding that he was closely followed, and that the hungry brother was approaching very fast, changed himself into a very old man, with two daughters, and living in a large lodge in the center of a beautiful garden, which was filled with every thing that could delight the eye, or was pleasant to the taste. He made himself appear so very old as to be unable to leave his lodge, and to require his daughters to bring him food and wait on him, as though he had been a mere child. The garden also had the appearance of old age, with its ancient bushes and hanging branches and decrepit vines loitering lazily about in the sun.

The brother kept on until he was nearly starved and ready to sink to the earth. He exclaimed, with a long-drawn and most mournful sigh, " Oh ! I will forget the blood of my sisters, for I am starving. Oh ! oh !"

But again he thought of the blood of his sisters, and what a fine appetite he would have if he should ever be allowed to eat any thing again, and once more he resolved to pursue, and to be content with nothing short of the amplest revenge.

He pushed on till he came to the beautiful garden. He advanced toward the lodge.

As soon as the fairy daughters perceived him they ran and told their father that a stranger approached.

Their father replied, " Invite him in, my children, invite him in."

They did so promptly, and, by the command of

their father, they boiled some corn, and prepared several other palatable dishes. The savor was most delicious to the nostrils of the hungry brother, who had not the least suspicion of the sport that was going on at his expense.

He was faint and weary with travel, and he felt that he could endure fasting no longer; for his appetite was terribly inflamed by the sight of the choice food that was steaming before him.

He fell to and partook heartily of the meal; and, by so doing, he was overcome, and lost his right of revenge. All at once he forgot the blood of his sisters, and even the village of his nativity, and his father's lodge, and his whole past life. He ate so keenly, and came and went to the choice dishes so often, that drowsiness at length overpowered him, and he soon fell into a profound sleep.

Onwee Bahmondang watched his opportunity, and as soon as he saw that the false brother's sleep was sound, he resumed his youthful form, and sent off the two fairy daughters and the old garden; and drawing the magic-ball from his back, which turned out to be a great war-club, he fetched the slumbering brother a mighty blow, which sent him away too; and thus did Onwee Bahmondang vindicate his title as the Wearer of the Ball.

When Onwee swung around, with the great force and weight of the club with which he had dispatched the brother of the two wicked women, he found himself in a large village, surrounded by a great crowd of people. At the door of a beautiful lodge stood his sister, smiling, and ready to invite him in. Onwee entered, and hanging up his war-club and the enchanted moccasins, which he had recovered, he rested from his labors, and smoked his evening pipe, with the admiration and appoval of the whole world.

With one exception only, Onwee Bahmondang had the hearty praises of all the people.

Now it happened that there lived in this same village an envious and boastful fellow, who had been once a chief, but coming home always badly whipped, he was put out of office, and now spent his time about the place mainly, in proclaiming certain great things which he had in his eye, and which he meant to do— one of these days.

This man's name was Ko-ko, the Owl; and hearing much of the wonderful achievements of the Wearer of the Ball, Ko-ko put on a big look, and announced that he was going to do something extraordinary himself.

Onwee Bahmondang, he said, had not half done his work, and he, Ko-ko, meant to go on the ground and finish it up as it should be.

He began by procuring an oak ball, which he thrust down his back, and, confident in its magical powers, he called himself, too, the Wearer of the

Ball. In fact it was the self-same ball that Onwee
had employed, except that the magic had entirely
gone out of it. Coming by night in the shadow of
the lodge, he thrust his arm in at the door, and stealthily possessed himself of the enchanted moccasins.
He would have taken away Onwee's war-club too, if
he could have carried it; but although he was twice
the size and girth of Onwee, he had not the strength
to lift it; so he borrowed a club from an old chief, who
was purblind, and mistook Ko-ko for his brother
who was a brave man; and raising a terrible tumult
with his voice, and a great dust with his heels, Ko-
ko set out.

He had traveled all day, when he came to a small
wigwam, and on looking into it, he discovered a very
old woman sitting alone by the fire; just as Onwee
had before.

This is the wigwam, said Ko-ko, and this is the
old woman.

" What are you looking for ?" asked the old woman.

" I want to find the lodge with the wicked young
women in it, who slay travellers and steal their trap-
pings," answered Ko-ko.

" You mean the two young women who lived in
the flying lodge ?" said the old woman.

" The same," answered Ko-ko. " I am going to
kill them."

With this he gave a great flourish with his bor-lowed club, and looked desperate and murderous as he could.

"They were slain yesterday by the Wearer of the Ball," said the old woman.

Ko-ko looked around for the door in a very owlish way, and heaving a short hem from his chest, he acknowledged that he had heard something to that effect down in one of the villages.

"But there's the brother. I'll have a chance at him," said Ko-ko.

"He is dead too," said the old woman.

"Is there nobody then left for me to kill?" cried Ko-ko. "Must I then go back without any blood upon my hands?"

He made as if he could shed tears over his sad mishap.

"The father is still living; and you will find him in the lodge, if you have a mind to call on him. He would like to see the Owl," the old woman added.

"He shall," replied Ko-ko. "Have you any bones about the house; for I suppose I shall have to climb that tree."

"Oh, yes; plenty," answered the old woman "You can have as many as you want."

And she gave him a handful of fish-bones, which Ko-ko, taking them to be the Invisible Tallies which had helped Onwee Bahmondang in climbing the magical tree, thrust into his bosom.

" Thank you," said Ko-ko, taking up his club and striding toward the door.

" Will you not have a little advice," said the old woman. " This is a dangerous business you are going on."

Ko-ko turned about and laughed to scorn the proposal, and putting forth his right foot from the lodge first, an observance in which he had great hopes, he started for the lodge of the wicked father.

Ko-ko ran very fast, as if he feared he should lose the chance of massacring any member of the wicked family, until he came in sight of the lodge hanging upon the tree.

He then slackened his pace, and crept forward with a wary eye lest somebody might chance to be looking out at the door. All was, however, still up there; and Ko-ko clasped the tree and began to climb.

Away went the lodge, and up went Ko-ko, puffing and panting, after it. And it was not a great while before the Owl had puffed and panted away all the wind he had to spare; and yet the lodge kept flying aloft, higher, higher. What was to be done!

Ko-ko of course bethought him of the bones, for that was just what, as he knew, had occurred to On-wee Bahmondang under the like circumstances.

He had the bones in his bosom; and now it was necessary for him to be a squirrel. He immediately called on several guardian spirits whom he knew of by name, and requested them to convert him into a squirrel. But not one of all them seemed to pay the slightest attention to his request; for there he hung, the same heavy-limbed, big-headed, be-clubbed, and be-blanketed Ko-ko as ever.

He then desired that they would turn him into an opossum; an application which met with the same luck as the previous one. After this he petitioned to be a wolf, a gophir, a dog, or a bear—if they would be so obliging. The guardian spirits were either all deaf, or indifferent to his wishes, or absent on some other business.

Ko-ko, in spite of all his begging and supplication and beseeching, was obliged to be still Ko-ko.

"The bones, however," he said to himself, "are good. I shall get a nice rest, at any rate, if I am forced to climb as I am."

With this he drew out one of the bones from his bosom, and shouting aloud, "Ho! ho! who is there?" he thrust it into the trunk of the tree, and would have indulged himself in a rest; but being no more than a common fish-bone, without the slightest savor of magic in it, it snapped with Ko-ko, who came tumbling down, with the door of the lodge which he had shaken loose, rattling after him.

"Ho! ho! who is there?" cried the wicked father, making his appearance at the opening and looking down.

"It is I, Onwee Bahmandang!" cried Ko-koor, thinking to frighten the wicked father.

"Ah! it is you, is it? I will be there presently," called the old man. "Do not be in haste to go away!'

"Ko-ko, observing that the old man was in earnest, scrambled up from the ground, and set off promptly at his highest rate of speed.

When he looked back and saw that the wicked father was gaining upon him, Ko-koor mounted a tree, as had Onwee Bahmandang before, and fired off a number of arrows, but as they were no more than common arrows, he got nothing by it, but was obliged to descend, and run again for life.

As he hurried on he encountered the skeleton of a moose, into which he would have transformed himself, but not having the slightest confidence in any one of all the guardians who should have helped him, he passed on.

The wicked father was hot in pursuit, and Ko-koor was suffering terribly for lack of wind, when luckily he remembered the enchanted moccasins. He could not send them to the end of the earth, as had Onwee Bahmondang.

"I will improve on that dull fellow," said Ko-ko. "I will put them on myself."

Accordingly, Ko-ko had just time to draw on the moccasins when the wicked father came in sight.

"Go now!" cried Ko-ko, giving orders to the enchanted moccasins; and go they did; but to the astonishment of the Owl, they turned immediately about in the way in which the wicked father, now very furious, was approaching.

"The other way! the other way!" cried Ko-ko.

Cry as loud as he would, the enchanted moccasins would keep on in their own course; and before he could shake himself out of them, they had run him directly into the face of the wicked father.

"What do you mean, you Owl?" cried the wicked father, falling upon Ko-ko with a huge club, and counting his ribs at every stroke.

"I can not help it, good man," answered Ko-ko. "I tried my best—"

Ko-ko would have gone the other way, but the enchanted moccasins kept hurrying him forward. "Stand off, will you?" cried the old man.

By this time, allowing the wicked father chance to bestow no more than five-and-twenty more blows upon Ko-ko, the moccasins were taking him past.

"Stop!" cried the old man again. "You are running away. Ho! ho! you are a coward!"

"I am not, good man," answered Ko-ko, carried away by the magical shoes, "I assure you." But ere he could finish his avowal, the moccasins had hurried him out of sight.

"At any rate, I shall soon be home at this speed,' said Ko-koor to himself.

The moccasins seemed to know his thoughts; for just then they gave a sudden leap, slipped away from his feet, and left the Owl flat upon his back! while they glided home by themselves, to the lodge of Onwee Bahmondang, where they belonged.

A party of hunters passing that way after several days, found Ko-ko sitting among the bushes, looking greatly bewildered; and when they inquired of him how he had succeeded with the wicked father at the lodge, he answered that he had demolished the whole establishment, but that his name was not Ko-ko, but Onwee Bahmondang; saying which, he ran away into the woods, and was never seen more.

XVII.

HE OF THE LITTLE SHELL.

ONCE upon a time, all the people of a certain country had died, excepting two helpless children, a baby boy and a little girl.

When their parents died, these children were asleep. The little girl, who was the elder, was the first to awake. She looked around her, but seeing nobody beside her little brother, who lay smiling in his dreams, she quietly resumed her bed.

At the end of ten days her brother moved, without opening his eyes.

At the end of ten days more he changed his position, lying on the other side, and in this way he kept on sleeping for a long time ; and pleasant, too, must have been his dreams, for his little sister never looked at him that he was not quite a little heaven of smiles and flashing lights, which beamed about his head and filled the lodge with a strange splendor.

The girl soon grew to be a woman, but the boy increased in stature very slowly. It was a long time before he could even creep, and he was well advanced in years before he could stand alone.   When he was able to walk, his sister made him a little bow and arrows, and hung around his neck a small shell, saying :

"You shall be called Dais Imid, or He of the Little Shell."

Every day he would go out with his little bow, shooting at the small birds.   The first bird he killed was a tom-tit.   His sister was highly pleased when he took it to her.   She carefully prepared and stuffed it, and put it away for him.

The next day he killed a red squirrel.   His sister preserved this, too.   The third day he killed a partridge, and this they had for their evening meal.

After this he acquired more courage, and would venture some distance from home.   His skill and success as a hunter daily increased, and he killed the deer, bear, moose, and other large animals inhabiting the forest.

At last, although so very small of stature, he became a great hunter, and all that he shot he brought home and shared with his sister ; and whenever he entered the lodge, a light beamed about his head and filled the place with a strange splendor.

He had now arrived at the years of manhood, but he still remained a perfect infant in size.

One day, walking about in quest of game, he came to a small lake.

It was in the winter season ; and upon the ice of

the lake he saw a man of giant height, employed killing beavers.

Comparing himself with this great man, he felt that he was no bigger than an insect. He seated himself on the shore and watched his movements.

When the large man had killed many beavers, he put them on a hand-sled which he had, and pursued his way home. When he saw him retire, the dwarf hunter followed, and, wielding his magic shell, he cut off the tail of one of the beavers, and ran home with the prize.

The giant, on reaching his lodge with his sled-load of beavers, was surprised to find one of them shorn of its tail.

The next day the little hero of the shell went to the same lake. The giant, who had been busy there for some time, had already loaded his sled and commenced his return ; but running nimbly forward and overtaking him, he succeeded in securing another of the beaver-tails.

" I wonder," said the giant, on reaching his lodge and overlooking his beavers, " what dog it is that has thus cheated me. Could I meet him, I would make his flesh quiver at the point of my javelin."

The giant forgot that he had taken these very beavers out of a beaver-dam which belonged to the little shell-man and his sister, without permission.

The next day he pursued his hunting at the beaver-dam near the lake, and he was again followed by the little man with the shell.

This time the giant was so nimble in his movements that he had nearly reached home before the Shell, make the best speed he could, could overtake him ; but he was just in time to clip another beaver's tail before the sled slipped into the lodge.

The giant would have been a patient giant, indeed, if his anger had not been violent at these constant tricks played upon him. What vexed him most, was, that he could not get a sight of his enemy. Sharp eyes he would have needed to do so, inasmuch as he of the little shell had the gift of making himself invisible whenever he chose.

The giant, giving vent to his feelings with many loud rumbling words, looked sharply around to see whether he could discover any tracks. He could find none. The unknown had stepped too lightly to leave the slightest mark behind.

The next day the giant resolved to disappoint his mysterious follower by going to the beaver-dam very early ; and accordingly, when the little shell man came to the place he found the fresh traces of his work, but the giant had already gone away. He followed hard upon his tracks, but he failed to overtake him. When he of the little shell came in sight of the lodge, the stranger was in front of it, employed in skinning his beavers.

As Dais-Imid stood looking at him—for he had
been all this time invisible—he thought :

"I will let him have a view of me."

Presently the man, who proved to be no less a per-
sonage than the celebrated giant, Manabozho, looked
up and saw him.

After regarding him with attention, "Who are
you, little man ?" said Manabozho. "I have a mind
to kill you."

The little hero of the shell replied :

"If you were to try to kill me you could not do it."

With this speech of the little man, Manabozho
grabbed at him ; but when he thought to have had
him in his hand, he was gone.

"Where are you now, little man ?" cried Manabozho.

"Here, under your girdle," answered the shell-
dwarf ; at which giant Manabozho, thinking to crush
him, slapped down his great hand with all his might;
but on unloosing his girdle he was disappointed at
finding no dwarf there.

"Where are you now, little man ?" he cried again,
in a greater rage than ever.

"In your right nostril !" the dwarf replied ; whereupon the giant Manabozho seized himself by the finger and thumb at the place, and gave it a violent
tweak ; but as he immediately heard the voice of
the dwarf at a distance upon the ground, he was sat-

isfied that he had only pulled his own nose to no pur·
pose.

"Good-by, Manabozho," said the voice of the invisible dwarf. "Count your beaver-tails, and you
will find that I have taken another for my sister ;"
for he of the little shell never, in his wanderings or
pastimes, forgot his sister and her wishes. "Good-
by, beaver-man !"

And as he went away he made himself visible
once more, and a light beamed about his head and
lit the air around him with a strange splendor ; a
circumstance which Manabozho, who was at times
quite thick-headed and dull of apprehension, could
no way understand.

When Dais-Imid returned home, he told his sister
that the time drew nigh when they must separate.

"I must go away," said Dais-Imid, "it is my
fate. You, too," he added, "must go away soon.
Tell me where you would wish to dwell."

She said, "I would like to go to the place of the
breaking of daylight. I have always loved the East.
The earliest glimpses of light are from that quarter,
and it is to my mind the most beautiful part of the
heavens. After I get there, my brother, whenever
you see the clouds, in that direction, of various colors,
you may think that your sister is painting her face."

"And I," said he, " I, my sister, shall live on the
mountains and rocks. There I can see you at the

THE MORNING STAR AND HER BROTHER. Page 212.

earliest hour ; there are the streams of water clear ; the air is pure, and the golden lights will shine ever around my head, and I shall ever be called ' Puck-Ininee, or the Little Wild Man of the Mountains.' But," he resumed, " before we part forever, I must go and try to find what manitoes rule the earth, and see which of them will be friendly to us."

He left his sister and traveled over the surface of the globe, and then went far down into the earth.

He had been treated well wherever he went. At last he came to a giant manito, who had a large kettle which was forever boiling. The giant, who was a first cousin to Manabozho, and had already heard of the tricks which Dais-Imid had played upon his kinsman, regarded him with a stern look, and, catching him up in his hand, he threw him unceremoniously into the kettle.

It was evidently the giant's intention to drown Dais-Imid ; in which he was mistaken, for by means of his magic shell, little Dais, in less than a second's time, bailed the water to the bottom, leaped from the kettle, and ran away unharmed.

He returned to his sister and related his rovings and adventures. He finished his story by addressing her thus :

" My sister there is a manito at each of the four corners of the earth. There is also one above them, far in the sky, a Great Being who assigns to you, and

to me, and to all of us, where we must go. And
last," he continued, "there is another and wicked
one who lives deep down in the earth. It will be our
lot to escape out of his reach. We must now separate. When the winds blow from the four corners
of the earth, you must then go. They will carry
you to the place you wish. I go to the rocks and
mountains, where my kindred will ever delight to
dwell."

Dais-Imid then took his ball-stick and commenced
running up a high mountain, and a bright light
shone about his head all the way, and he kept singing as he went :

Blow, winds, blow ! my sister lingers
    For her dwelling in the sky,
Where the morn, with rosy fingers,
    Shall her cheeks with vermil dye.

There my earliest views directed,
    Shall from her their color take,
And her smiles, through clouds reflected,
    Guide me on by wood or lake.

While I range the highest mountains,
    Sport in valleys green and low,
Or, beside our Indian fountains,
    Raise my tiny hip-hallo.

Presently the winds blew, and, as Dais-Imid had
predicted, his sister was borne by them to the eastern sky, where she has ever since lived, and her name
is now the Morning Star.

XVIII.

MANABOZHO, THE MISCHIEF-MAKER.

THERE was never in the whole world a more mischievous busy-body than that notorious giant Manabozho. He was every where, in season and out of season, running about, and putting his hand in whatever was going forward. To carry on his game, he could take almost any shape he pleased; he could be very foolish or very wise; very weak or very strong; very poor or very rich—just as happened to suit his humor best. Whatever any one else could do, he would attempt without a moment's reflection. He was a match for any man he met, and there were few manitoes that could get the better of him. By turns he would be very kind, or very cruel; an animal or a bird; a man or a spirit; and yet, in spite of all these gifts, Manabozho was always getting himself involved in all sorts of troubles; and more than once, in the course of his busy adventures, was this great maker of mischief driven to his wits' ends to come off with his life.

To begin at the beginning, Manabozho, while yet a youngster, was living with his grandmother, near the edge of a wide prairie. It was on this prairie that he first saw animals and birds of every kind ; he also there made first acquaintance with thunder and lightning; he would sit by the hour watching the clouds as they rolled, and musing on the shades of light and darkness as the day rose and fell.

For a stripling, Manabozho was uncommonly wide-awake. Every new sight he beheld in the heavens was a subject of remark; every new animal or bird, an object of deep interest; and every sound that came from the bosom of nature, was like a new lesson which he was expected to learn. He often trembled at what he heard and saw.

To the scene of the wide open prairie his grandmother sent him at an early age to watch. The first sound he heard was that of the owl, at which he was greatly terrified, and, quickly descending the tree he had climbed, he ran with alarm to the lodge. "Noko ! noko ! grandmother!" he cried. "I have heard a monedo."

She laughed at his fears, and asked him what kind of noise his reverence made. He answered, "It makes a noise like this : ko-ko-ko-ho."

His grandmother told him he was young and foolish; that what he heard was only a bird which derived its name from the peculiar noise it made.

He returned to the prairie and continued his watch. As he stood there looking at the clouds, he thought to himself, "It is singular that I am so simple and my grandmother so wise; and that I have neither father nor mother. I have never heard a word about them. I must ask and find out."

He went home and sat down, silent and dejected. Finding that this did not attract the notice of his grandmother, he began a loud lamentation, which he kept increasing, louder and louder, till it shook the lodge, and nearly deafened the old grandmother. She at length said, "Manabozho, what is the matter with you? you are making a great deal of noise."

Manabozho started off again with his doleful hub-bub; but succeeded in jerking out between his big sobs, "I have n't got any father nor mother; I have n't;" and he set out again lamenting more boisterously than ever.

Knowing that he was of a wicked and revengeful temper, his grandmother dreaded to tell him the story of his parentage; as she knew he would make trouble of it.

Manabozho renewed his cries, and managed to throw out, for a third or fourth time, his sorrowful lament that he was a poor unfortunate, who had no parents and no relations.

She at last said to him, "Yes, you have a father and three brothers living. Your mother is dead. She was taken for a wife by your father, the West without the consent of her parents. Your brothers are the North, East, and South; and being older than yourself, your father has given them great power with the winds, according to their names. You are the youngest of his children. I have nursed you from your infancy; for your mother, owing to the ill-treatment of your father, died in giving you birth. I have no relations beside you this side of the planet in which I was born, and from which I was precipitated by female jealousy. Your mother was my only child, and you are my only hope."

"I am glad my father is living," said Manabozho. "I shall set out in the morning to visit him."

His grandmother would have discouraged him; saying it was a long distance to the place where his father, Ningabiun, or the West, lived.

This information seemed rather to please than to disconcert Manabozho; for by this time he had grown to such a size and strength that he had been compelled to leave the narrow shelter of his grandmother's lodge and to live out of doors. He was so tall that, if he had been so disposed, he could have snapped off the heads of the birds roosting in the topmost branches of the highest trees, as he stood up, without being at the trouble to climb. And if he had at any time taken a fancy to one of the same trees for a walking-stick, he would have had no more to do than to pluck it up with his thumb and finger, and strip down the leaves and twigs with the palm of his hand.

Bidding good-by to his venerable old grandmother, who pulled a very long face over his departure, Manabozho set out at great headway, for he was able to stride from one side of a prairie to the other at a single step.

He found his father on a high mountain-ground, far in the west. His father espied his approach at a great distance, and bounded down the mountain-side several miles to give him welcome, and, side-by-side, apparently delighted with each other, they reached in two or three of their giant paces the lodge of the West, which stood high up near the clouds.

They spent some days in talking with each other —for these two great persons did nothing on a small scale, and a whole day to deliver a single sentence, such was the immensity of their discourse, was quite an ordinary affair.

One evening, Manabozho asked his father what he was most afraid of on earth.

He replied—" Nothing."

" But is there nothing you dread, here—nothing that would hurt you if you took too much of it ? Come, tell me."

Manabozho was very urgent ; at last his father said:

" Yes, there is a black stone to be found a couple

of hundred miles from here, over that way," pointing as he spoke. " It is the only thing earthly that I am afraid of, for if it should happen to hit me on any part of my body it would hurt me very much."

The West made this important circumstance known to Manabozho in the strictest confidence.

" Now you will not tell any one, Manabozho, that the black stone is bad medicine for your father, will you ?" he added. " You are a good son, and I know will keep it to yourself. Now tell me, my darling boy, is there not something that you don't like ?"

Manabozho answered promptly—" Nothing."

His father, who was of a very steady and persevering temper, put the same question to him seventeen times, and each time Manabozho made the same answer—" Nothing."

But the West insisted—" There must be something you are afraid of."

" Well, I will tell you," says Manabozho, " what it is."

He made an effort to speak, but it seemed to be too much for him.

" Out with it," said Ningabiun, or the West, fetching Manabozho such a blow on the back as shook the mountain with its echo.

" Je-ee, je-ee—it is," said Manabozho, apparently in great pain. " Yeo, yeo ! I can not name it, I tremble so."

The West told him to banish his fears, and to speak up ; no one would hurt him.

Manabozho began again, and he would have gone over the same make-believe of anguish, had not his father, whose strength he knew was more than a match for his own, threatened to pitch him into a river about five miles off. At last he cried out :

" Father, since you will know, it is the root of the bulrush."

He who could with perfect ease spin a sentence a whole day long, seemed to be exhausted by the effort of pronouncing that one word, " bulrush."

Some time after, Manabozho observed :

" I will get some of the black rock, merely to see how it looks."

" Well," said the father, " I will also get a little of the bulrush-root, to learn how it tastes."

They were both double-dealing with each other, and in their hearts getting ready for some desperate work.

They had no sooner separated for the evening than Manabozho was striding off the couple of hundred miles necessary to bring him to the place where black rock was to be procured, while down the other side of the mountain hurried Ningabiun.

At the break of day they each appeared at the great level on the mountain-top, Manabozho with twenty loads, at least, of the black stone, on one side, and on the other the West, with a whole meadow of bulrush in his arms.

Manabozho was the first to strike—hurling a great piece of the black rock, which struck the West directly between the eyes, who returned the favor with a blow of bulrush, that rung over the shoulders of Manabozho, far and wide, like the whip-thong of the lightning among the clouds.

And now either rallied, and Manabozho poured in a tempest of black rock, while Ningabiun discharged a shower of bulrush. Blow upon blow, thwack upon thwack—they fought hand to hand until black rock and bulrush were all gone. Then they betook themselves to hurling crags at each other, cudgeling with huge oak-trees, and defying each other from one mountain-top to another; while at times they shot enormous boulders of granite across at each other's heads, as though they had been mere jack-stones. The battle, which had commenced on the mountains, had extended far west. The West was forced to give ground. Manabozho pressing on, drove him across rivers and mountains, ridges and lakes, till at last he got him to the very brink of the world.

"Hold!" cried the West. "My son, you know my power, and although I allow that I am now fairly out of breath, it is impossible to kill me. Stop where you are, and I will also portion you out with as much power as your brothers. The four quarters of the globe are already occupied, but you can go and do a great deal of good to the people of the earth, which is beset with serpents, beasts and monsters, who make great havoc of human life. Go and do good, and if you put forth half the strength you have to-day, you will acquire a name that will last forever. When you have finished your work I will have a place provided for you. You will then go and sit with your brother, Kabinocca, in the North."

Manabozho gave his father his hand upon this agreement. And parting from him, he returned to his own grounds, where he lay for some time sore of his wounds.

These being, however, greatly allayed, and soon after cured by his grandmother's skill in medicines, Manabozho, as big and sturdy as ever, was ripe for new adventures. He set his thoughts immediately upon a war excursion against the Pearl Feather, a wicked old manito, living on the other side of the great lake, who had killed his grandfather. He begun his preparations by making huge bows and arrows without number; but he had no heads for his shafts. At last Noko told him that an old man, who lived at some distance, could furnish him with such as he needed. He sent her to get some. She soon returned with her wrapper full. Manabozho told her that he had not enough, and sent her again. She came back with as many more. He thought to himself, "I must find out the way of making these heads."

Instead of directly asking how it was done, he preferred—just like Manabozho—to deceive his grandmother to come at the knowledge he desired, by a trick. "Noko," said he, "while I take my drum and rattle, and sing my war-songs, do you go and try to get me some larger heads, for these you have brought me are all of the same size. Go and see whether the old man is not willing to make some a little larger."

He followed her at a distance as she went, having left his drum at the lodge, with a great bird tied at the top, whose fluttering should keep up the drumbeat, the same as if he were tarrying at home. He saw the old workman busy, and learned how he prepared the heads; he also beheld the old man's daughter, who was very beautiful; and Manabozho now discovered for the first time that he had a heart of his own, and the sigh he heaved passed through the arrow-maker's lodge like a gale of wind.

"How it blows!" said the old man.

"It must be from the south," said the daughter; "for it is very fragrant."

Manabozho slipped away, and in two strides he was at home, shouting forth his songs as though he had never left the lodge. He had just time to free the bird which had been beating the drum, when his grandmother came in and delivered to him the big arrow-heads.

In the evening the grandmother said, "My son, you ought to fast before you go to war, as your brothers do, to find out whether you will be successful or not."

He said he had no objection; and having privately stored away, in a shady place in the forest, two or three dozen juicy bears, a moose, and twenty strings of the tenderest birds, he would retire from the lodge so far as to be entirely out of view of his grandmother, fall to and enjoy himself heartily, and at nightfall, having just dispatched a dozen birds and half a bear or so, he would return, tottering and wo-begone, as if quite famished, so as to move deeply the sympathies of his wise old granddame.

The place of his fast had been chosen by the Noko, and she had told him it must be so far as to be beyond the sound of her voice or it would be unlucky.

After a time Manabozho, who was always spying out mischief, said to himself, "I must find out why my grandmother is so anxious to have me fast at this spot."

The next day he went but a short distance. She cried out, "A little further off;" but he came nearer to the lodge, the rogue that he was, and cried out in a low, counterfeited voice, to make it appeaı that he was going away instead of approaching. He had now got so near that he could see all that passed in the lodge,

He had not been long in ambush when an old magician crept into the lodge. This old magician had very long hair, which hung across his shoulders and down his back, like a bush or foot-mat. They commenced talking about him, and in doing so, they put their two old heads so very close together that Manabozho was satisfied they were kissing each other. He was indignant that any one should take such a liberty with his venerable grandmother, and to mark his sense of the outrage, he touched the bushy hair of the old magician with a live coal which he had blown upon. The old magician had not time to kiss the old grandmother more than once again before he felt the flame; and jumping out into the air, it burned only the fiercer, and he ran, blazing like a fire-ball, across the prairie.

Manabozho who had, meanwhile, stolen off to his fasting-place, cried out, in a heart-broken tone, and as if on the very point of starvation, "Noko! Noko! is it time for me to come home?"

"Yes," she cried. And when he came in she asked him, "Did you see any thing?"

"Nothing," he answered, with an air of childish candor; looking as much like a big simpleton as he could   The grandmother looked at him very closely and said no more.

Manabozho finished his term of fasting; in the course of which he slyly dispatched twenty fat bears, six dozen birds, and two fine moose; sung his war-song, and embarked in his canoe, fully prepared for war.   Beside weapons of battle, he had stowed in a large supply of oil.

He traveled rapidly night and day, for he had only to will or speak, and the canoe went.   At length he arrived in sight of the fiery serpents.   He paused to view them; he observed that they were some distance apart, and that the flames which they constantly belched forth reached across the pass.   He gave them a good morning, and began talking with them in a very friendly way; but they answered, " We know you, Manabozho; you can not pass."

He was not, however, to be put off so easily.   Turning his canoe as if about to go back, he suddenly cried out with a loud and terrified voice :

" What is that behind you ?"

The serpents, thrown off their guard, instantly turned their heads, and he in a moment glided past them.

" Well," said he, quietly, after he had got by, " how do you like my movement ?"

He then took up his bow and arrows, and with deliberate aim shot every one of them, easily, for the serpents were fixed to one spot, and could not even turn around. They were of an enormous length, and of a bright color.

Having thus escaped the sentinel serpents, Manabozho pushed on in his canoe until he came to a part of the lake called Pitch-water, as whatever touched it was sure to stick fast. But Manabozho was prepared with his oil, and rubbing his canoe freely from end to end, he slipped through with ease, and he was the first person who had ever succeeded in passing through the Pitch-water.

"There is nothing like a little oil to help one through pitch-water," said Manabozho to himself.

Now in view of land, he could see the lodge of the Shining Manito, high upon a distant hill.

Putting his clubs and arrows in order, just at the dawn of day Manabozho began his attack, yelling and shouting, and beating his drum, and calling out in triple voices :

"Surround him ! surround him ! run up ! run up !" making it appear that he had many followers. He advanced, shouting aloud :

"It was you that killed my grandfather," and shot off a whole forest of arrows.

The Pearl Feather appeared on the height, blazing like the sun, and paid back the discharges of Manabozho with a tempest of bolts, which rattled like the hail.

All day long the fight was kept up, and Manabozho had fired all of his arrows but three, without
effect ; for the Shining Manito was clothed in pure
wampum. It was only by immense leaps to right
and left that Manabozho could save his head from
the sturdy blows which fell about him on every side,
like pine-trees, from the hands of the Manito. He
was badly bruised, and at his very wit's end, when a
large wood-pecker flew past and lit on a tree. It
was a bird he had known on the prairie, near his
grandmother's lodge.

" Manabozho," called out the wood-pecker, " your
enemy has a weak point ; shoot at the lock of hair on
the crown of his head."

He shot his first arrow and only drew blood in a
few drops. The Manito made one or two unsteady
steps, but recovered himself. He began to parley,
but Manabozho, now that he had discovered a way to
reach him, was in no humor to trifle, and he let slip
another arrow, which brought the Shining Manito
to his knees. And now, having the crown of his
head within good range, Manabozho sent in his third
arrow, which laid the Manito out upon the ground,
stark dead.

Manabozho lifted up a huge war-cry, beat his
drum, took the scalp of the Manito as his trophy,
and calling the wood-pecker to come and receive a re-
ward for the timely hint he had given him, he rubbed

the blood of the Shining Manito on the wood-pecker's head, the feathers of which are red to this day.
Full of his victory, Manabozho returned home, beating his war-drum furiously, and shouting aloud his
songs of triumph. His grandmother was on the
shore ready to welcome him with the war-dance,
which she performed with wonderful skill for one so
far advanced in years.

The heart of Manabozho swelled within him. He
was fairly on fire, and an unconquerable desire for further adventures seized upon him. He had destroyed
the powerful Pearl Feather, killed his serpents, and
escaped all his wiles and charms. He had prevailed
in a great land fight, his next trophy should be from
the water.

He tried his prowess as a fisherman, and with such
success that he captured a fish so monstrous in size
and so rich in fat that with the oil Manabozho was
able to form a small lake. To this, being generously
disposed, and having a cunning purpose of his own
to answer, he invited all the birds and beasts of his
acquaintance ; and he made the order in which
they partook of the banquet the measure of their fat-
ness for all time to come. As fast as they arrived he
told them to plunge in and help themselves.

The first to make his appearance was the bear,
who took a long and steady draught ; then came the
deer, the opossum, and such others of the family as

are noted for their comfortable case. The moose and bison were slack in their cups, and the partridge, always lean in flesh, looked on till the supply was nearly gone. There was not a drop left by the time the hare and the martin appeared on the shore of the lake, and they are, in consequence, the slenderest of all creatures.

When this ceremony was over, Manabozho suggested to his friends, the assembled birds and animals, that the occasion was proper for a little merry-making; and taking up his drum, he cried out:

"New songs from the South, come, brothers, dance!"

He directed them, to make the sport more mirthful, that they should shut their eyes and pass around him in a circle. Again he beat his drum and cried out:

"New songs from the South, come, brothers, dance!"

They all fell in and commenced their rounds. Whenever Manabozho, as he stood in the circle, saw a fat fowl which he fancied, pass by him, he adroitly wrung its neck and slipped it in his girdle, at the same time beating his drum and singing at the top of his lungs, to drown the noise of the fluttering, and crying out in a tone of admiration:

"That's the way, my brothers; that's the way!"

At last a small duck, of the diver family, thinking

there was something wrong, opened one eye and saw what Manabozho was doing. Giving a spring, and crying :

"Ha-ha-a ! Manabozho is killing us !" he made fo- the water.

Manabozho, quite vexed that the creature should have played the spy upon his house-keeping, followed him, and just as the diver-duck was getting into the water, gave him a kick, which is the reason that the diver's tail-feathers are few, his back flattened, and his legs straightened out, so that when he gets on land he makes a poor figure in walking.

Meantime, the other birds, having no ambition to be thrust in Manabozho's girdle, flew off, and the animals scampered into the woods.

Manabozho stretching himself at ease in the shade along the side of the prairie, thought what he should do next. He concluded that he would travel and see new countries; and having once made up his mind, in less than three days, such was his length of limb and the immensity of his stride, he had walked over the entire continent, looked into every lodge by the way, and with such nicety of observation, that he was able to inform his good old grandmother what each family had for a dinner at a given hour.

By way of relief to these grand doings, Manabozho was disposed to vary his experiences by bestowing a little time upon the sports of the woods. He had heard reported great feats in hunting, and he had a desire to try his power in that way.   Besides that, it was a slight consideration that he had devoured all the game within reach of the lodge; and so, one evening, as he was walking along the shore of the great lake, weary and hungry, he encountered a great magician in the form of an old wolf, with six young ones, coming toward him.

The wolf no sooner caught sight of him than he told his whelps, who were close about his side, to keep out of the way of Manabozho; " For I know," he said, " that it is that mischievous fellow whom we see yonder."

The young wolves were in the act of running off, when Manabozho cried out, " My grandchildren, where are you going?   Stop and I will go with you.   I wish to have a little chat with your excellent father."

Saying which he advanced and greeted the old wolf, expressing himself as delighted at seeing him looking so well.   " Whither do you journey?" he asked.

" We are looking for a good hunting-ground to pass the winter," the old wolf answered.   " What brings you here?"

" I was looking for you," said Manabozho.   " For I have a passion for the chase, brother.   I always admired your family; are you willing to change me into a wolf?"

The wolf gave him a favorable answer, and he was forthwith changed into a wolf.

" Well, that will do," said Manabozho; then looking at his tail, he added, " Oh! could you oblige me by making my tail a little longer and more bushy."

" Certainly," said the old wolf; and he gave Manabozho such a length and spread of tail, that it was constantly getting between his legs, and it was so heavy that it was as much as he could do to find strength to carry it. But having asked for it, he was ashamed to say a word; and they all started off in company, dashing up a ravine.

After getting into the woods for some distance, they fell in with the tracks of moose. The young ones scampered off in pursuit, the old wolf and Manabozho following at their leisure.

" Well," said the old wolf, by way of opening discourse, " who do you think is the fastest of the boys? Can you tell by the jumps they take?"

" Why," he replied, " that one that takes such long jumps, he is the fastest to be sure."

" Ha! ha! you are mistaken," said the old wolf. " He makes a good start, but he will be the first to tire out; this one, who appears to be behind, will be the one to kill the game."

By this time they had come to the spot where the boys had started in chase. One had dropped what seemed to be a small medicine-sack, which he carried for the use of the hunting-party.

" Take that, Manabozho," said the old wolf.

" Esa," he replied, " what will I do with a dirty dog-skin?"

The old wolf took it up; it was a beautiful robe.

" Oh, I will carry it now," cried Manabozho.

" Oh, no," said the old wolf, who had exerted his magical powers, " it is a robe of pearls. Come along !" And away sped the old wolf at a great rate of speed.

" Not so fast," called Manabozho after him; and then he added to himself as he panted after, " Oh, this tail !"

Coming to a place where the moose had lain down, they saw that the young wolves had made a fresh start after their prey.

" Why," said the old wolf, " this moose is poor. I know by the tracks; for I can always tell whether they are fat or not."

A little further on, one of the young wolves, in dashing at the moose, had broken a tooth on a tree.

" Manabozho," said the old wolf, " one of your grandchildren has shot at the game. Take his arrow; there it is."

" No," replied Manabozho; " what will I do with a dirty dog's tooth?"

The old wolf took it up, and behold it was a beautiful silver arrow.

When they at last overtook them, they found that the youngsters had killed a very fat moose. Manabozho was very hungry; but the old wolf just then again exerted his magical powers, and Manabozho saw nothing but the bones picked quite clean. He thought to himself, "Just as I expected; dirty, greedy fellows. If it had not been for this log at my back, I should have been in time to have got a mouthful:" and he cursed the bushy tail which he carried, to the bottom of his heart. He, however, sat down without saying a word.

At length the old wolf spoke to one of the young ones, saying :

" Give some meat to your grandfather."

One of them obeyed, and coming near to Manabozho, he presented him the other end of his own bushy tail, which was nicely seasoned with burs, gathered in the course of the hunt.

Manabozho jumped up and called out :

" You dog, now that your stomach is full, do you think I am going to eat you to get at my dinner ? Get you gone into some other place."

Saying which Manabozho, in his anger, walked off by himself.

" Come back, brother," cried the wolf.   " You are losing your eyes."

Manabozho turned back.

" You do the child injustice. Look there !" and

behold, a heap of fresh, ruddy meat, was lying on the spot, already prepared.

Manabozho, at the view of so much good provision, put on a smiling face.

" Amazement !" he said ; " how fine the meat is !'

" Yes," replied the old wolf, " it is always so with us ; we know our work, and always get the best. It is not a long tail that makes the hunter."

Manabozho bit his lip.

They now fixed their winter quarters. The youngsters went out in search of game, and they soon brought in a large supply. One day, during the absence of the young hunters, the old wolf amused himself in cracking the large bones of a moose.

" Manabozho," said he, " cover your head with the robe, and do not look at me while I am busy with these bones, for a piece may fly in your eye."

He did as he was bid ; but looking through a rent that was in the robe, he saw what the other was about. Just at that moment a piece flew off and hit him on the eye. He cried out :

" Tyau, why do you strike me, you old dog ?"

The wolf answered—" You must have been looking at me."

" No, no," retorted Manabozho, " why should I want to look at you ?"

" Manabozho," said the old wolf, " you must have been looking or you would not have got hurt."

"No, no," he replied again, "I was not. I will repay the saucy wolf this mischief," he thought to himself.

So the next day, taking up a bone to obtain the marrow, he said to the wolf:

"Brother, cover your head and do not look at me, for I very much fear a piece may fly in your eye."

The wolf did so; and Manabozho, taking the large leg-bone of the moose, first looking to see if the wolf was well covered, hit him a blow with all his might. The wolf jumped up, cried out, and fell prostrate from the effects of the blow.

"Why," said he, when he came to a little and was able to sit up, "why do you strike me so?"

"Strike you?" said Manabozho, with well-feigned surprise, "no; you must have been looking at me."

"No," answered the wolf, "I say I have not."

But Manabozho insisted, and as the old wolf was no great master of tricky argument, he was obliged to give it up.

Shortly after this the old wolf suggested to Manabozho that he should go out and try his luck in hunting by himself.

When he chose to put his mind upon it he was quite expert, and this time he succeeded in killing a fine fat moose, which he thought he would take aside slyly, and devour alone, having prepared to tell the old wolf a pretty story on his return, to account for his failure to bring any thing with him.

He was very hungry, and he sat down to eat ; but as he never could go to work in a straight-forward way, he immediately fell into great doubts as to the proper point at which to begin.

" Well," said he, " I do not know where to commence. At the head ? No. People will laugh, and say—' He ate him backward.' "

He went to the side. " No," said he, " they will say I ate him sideways."

He then went to the hind-quarter. " No, that will not do, either ; they will say I ate him forward. I will begin here, say what they will."

He took a delicate piece from the small of the back, and was just on the point of putting it to his mouth, when a tree close by made a creaking noise. He seemed vexed at the sound. He raised the morsel to his mouth the second time, when the tree creaked again.

" Why," he exclaimed, " I can not eat when I hear such a noise. Stop, stop !" he said to the tree. He put it down, exclaiming—" I can not eat with such a noise ;" and starting away he climbed the tree, and was pulling at the limb which had offended him, when his fore-paw was caught between the branches so that he could not free himself.

While thus held fast, he saw a pack of wolves advancing through the wood in the direction of his meat. He suspected them to be the old wolf and his cubs, but night was coming on and he could not make them out.

" Go the other way, go the other way !" he cried out ; " what would you come to get here ?"

The wolves stopped for a while and talked among themselves, and said :

" Manabozho must have something there, or he would not tell us to go another way."

" I begin to know him," said an old wolf, " and all his tricks. Let us go forward and see."

They came on, and finding the moose, they soon made away with it. Manabozho looked wistfully on to see them eat till they were fully satisfied, when they scampered off in high spirits.

A heavy blast of wind opened the branches and released Manabozho, who found that the wolves had left nothing but the bare bones. He made for home, where, when he related his mishap, the old wolf, taking him by the fore-paw, condoled with him deeply on his ill-luck. A tear even started to his eye as he added :

" My brother, this should teach us not to meddle with points of ceremony when we have good meat to eat."

The winter having by this time drawn fairly to a close, on a bright morning in the early spring, the old wolf addressed Manabozho: " My brother, I am obliged to leave you; and although I have sometimes been merry at your expense, I will show that I care for your comfort. I shall leave one of the boys behind me to be your hunter, and to keep you company through the long summer afternoons."

The old wolf galloped off with his five young ones; and as they disappeared from view, Manabozho was disenchanted in a moment, and returned to his mortal shape.

Although he had been sometimes vexed and imposed upon, he had, altogether, passed a pleasant winter with the cunning old wolf, and now that he was gone, Manabozho was downcast and low in spirit. But as the days grew brighter he recovered by degrees his air of cheerful confidence, and was ready to try his hand upon any new adventure that might occur to him. The old spirit of mischief was still alive within him.

The young wolf who had been left with him was a good hunter, and never failed to keep the lodge well supplied with meat. One day Manabozho addressed him as follows :

" My grandson, I had a dream last night, and it does not portend good. It is of the large lake which lies in that direction. You must be careful to always go across it, whether the ice seem strong or not. Never go around it, for there are enemies on the

11

further shore who lie in wait for you. The ice is always safe."

Now Manabozho knew well that the ice was thinning every day under the warm sun, but he could not stay himself from playing a trick upon the young wolf.

In the evening when he came to the lake, after a long day's travel in quest of game, the young wolf, confiding in his grandfather, said, "Hwooh! the ice does look thin, but Nesho says it is sound;" and he trotted upon the glassy plain.

He had not got half way across when the ice snapped, and with a mournful cry, the young wolf fell in and was immediately seized by the water-serpents who knew that it was Manabozho's grandson, and were thirsting for revenge upon him for the death of their relations in the war upon Pearl Feather.

Manabozho heard the young wolf's cry as he sat in his lodge; he knew what had happened; and, from that moment, he was deprived of the greater part of his magical power.

He returned, scarcely more than an ordinary mortal, to his former place of dwelling, whence his grandmother had departed no one knew whither. He married the arrow-maker's daughter, and became the father of several children, and very poor. He was scarcely able to procure the means of living. His lodge was pitched in a remote part of the country, where he could get no game. It was winter, and he had not the common comforts of life. He said to his wife one day, " I will go out a walking and see if I can not find some lodges."

After walking some time he saw a lodge at a distance. The children were playing at the door. When they saw him approaching they ran in and told their parents that Manabozho was coming.

It was the residence of the large red-headed woodpecker. He came to the door and asked Manabozho to enter. This invitation was promptly accepted.

After some time, the woodpecker, who was a magician, said to his wife :

" Have you nothing to give Manabozho ? he must be hungry."

She answered, " No."

" He ought not to go without his supper," said the woodpecker. " I will see what I can do."

In the center of the lodge stood a large tamarack-tree. Upon this the woodpecker flew, and commenced going up, turning his head on each side of the tree, and every now and then driving in his bill. At last he pulled something out of the tree and threw it down; when, behold, a fine fat raccoon lay on the ground. He drew out six or seven more. He then descended, and told his wife to prepare them.

" Manabozho," he said, " this is the only thing we eat; what else can we give you ?'

"It is very good," replied Manabozho.

They smoked their pipes and conversed with each other.

After eating, Manabozho got ready to go home; when the woodpecker said to his wife, "Give him the other raccoons to take home for his children."

In the act of leaving the lodge, Manabozho, on purpose, dropped one of his mittens, which was soon after observed upon the ground.

"Run," said the woodpecker to his eldest son, "and give it to him; but mind that you do not give it into his hand; throw it at him, for there is no knowing him, he acts so curiously."

The boy did as he was directed.

"Grandfather," said he to Manabozho, as he came up to him, "you have left one of your mittens; here it is."

"Yes," he said, affecting to be ignorant of the circumstance, "it is so; but don't throw it, you will soil it on the snow."

The lad, however, threw it, and was about to return, when Manabozho cried out, "Bakah! Bakah! stop—stop; is that all you eat? Do you eat nothing else with your raccoon? tell me!"

"Yes, that is all," answered the young Woodpecker; "we have nothing else."

"Tell your father," continued Manabozho, "to come and visit me, and let him bring a sack. I will give him what he shall eat with his raccoon-meat."

When the young one returned and reported this message to his father, the old woodpecker turned up his nose at the invitation. "I wonder," he said, "what he thinks he has got, poor fellow!"

He was bound, however, to answer the proffer of hospitality, and he went accordingly, taking along a cedar-sack, to pay a visit to Manabozho.

Manabozho received the old red-headed wood-pecker with great ceremony. He had stood at the door awaiting his arrival, and as soon as he came in sight Manabozho commenced, while he was yet far off, bowing and opening wide his arms, in token of welcome; all of which the woodpecker returned in due form, by ducking his bill, and hopping to right and left, upon the ground, extending his wings to their full length and fluttering them back to his breast.

When the woodpecker at last reached the lodge, Manabozho made various remarks upon the weather, the appearance of the country, and especially on the scarcity of game.

"But we," he added, "we always have enough. Come in, and you shall not go away hungry, my no-ble bird!"

Manabozho had always prided himself on being able to give as good as he had received; and to be up with the woodpecker, he had shifted his lodge so as to inclose a large dry tamarack-tree.

"What can I give you," said he to the wood-pecker; "but as we eat so shall you eat."

With this he hopped forward, and, jumping on the tamarack-tree, he attempted to climb it just as he had seen the woodpecker do in his own lodge. He turned his head first on one side, then on the other, in the manner of the bird, meanwhile striving to go up, and as often slipping down. Ever and anon he would strike the tree with his nose, as if it had been a bill, and draw back, but he pulled out no raccoons; and he dashed his nose so often against the trunk that at last the blood began to flow, and he tumbled down senseless upon the ground.

The woodpecker started up with his drum and rattle to restore him, and by beating them violently he succeeded in bringing him to.

As soon as he came to his senses, Manabozho began to lay the blame of his failure upon his wife, saying to his guest:

"Nemesho, it is this woman-relation of yours—she is the cause of my not succeeding. She has made me a worthless fellow. Before I took her I also could get raccoons."

The woodpecker said nothing, but flying on the tree he drew out several fine raccoons.

"Here," said he, "this is the way we do!" and

left him in disdain, carrying his bill high in the air, and stepping over the door-sill as if it were not worthy to be touched by his toes.

After this visit, Manabozho was sitting in the lodge one day with his head down. He heard the wind whistling around it, and thought that by attentively listening he could hear the voice of some one speaking to him. It seemed to say to him :

" Great chief, why are you sorrowful ? Am not I your friend—your guardian spirit ?"

Manabozho immediately took up his rattle, and without rising from the ground where he was sitting, began to sing the chant which has at every close the refrain of, " Wha lay le aw."

When he had dwelt for a long time on this peculiar chant, which he had been used to sing in all his times of trouble, he laid his rattle aside and determined to fast. For this purpose he went to a cave which faced the setting sun, and built a very small fire, near which he lay down, first telling his wife that neither she nor the children must come near him till he had finished his fast.

At the end of seven days he came back to the lodge, pale and thin, looking like a spirit himself, and as if he had seen spirits. His wife had in the meantime dug through the snow and got a few of the root called truffles. These she boiled and set before him, and this was all the food they had or seemed likely to obtain.

When he had finished his light repast, Manabozho took up his station in the door to see what would happen. As he stood thus, holding in his hand his large bow, with a quiver well filled with arrows, a deer glided past along the far edge of the prairie, but it was miles away, and no shaft that Manabozho could shoot would be able to touch it.

Presently a cry came down the air, and looking up he beheld a great flight of birds, but they were so far up in the sky that he would have lost his arrows in a vain attempt among the clouds.

Still he stood watchful, and confident that some turn of luck was about to occur, when there came near to the lodge two hunters, who bore between them on poles upon their shoulders, a bear, and it was so fine and fat a bear that it was as much as the two hunters could do with all their strength to carry it.

As they came to the lodge-door, one of the hunters asked if Manabozho lived thereabout.

" He is here," answered Manabozho.

" I have often heard of you," said the first hunter, " and I was curious to see you. But you have lost your magical power. Do you know whether any of it is left ?"

Manabozho answered that he was himself in the dark on the subject.

"Suppose you make a trial," said the hunter.

"What shall I do?" asked Manabozho.

"There is my friend," said the hunter, pointing to his companion, "who with me owns this bear which we are carrying home. Suppose you see if you can change him into a piece of rock."

"Very well," said Manabozho; and he had scarcely spoken before the other hunter became a rock.

"Now change him back again," said the first hunter.

"That I can't do," Manabozho answered; "there my power ends."

The hunter looked at the rock with a bewildered face.

"What shall I do?" he asked. "This bear I can never carry alone, and it was agreed between my friend there and myself, that we should not divide it till we reached home. Can't you change my friend back, Manabozho?"

"I would like to oblige you," answered Manabozho, "but it is utterly out of my power."

With this, looking again at the rock with a sad and bewildered face, and then casting a sorrowful glance at the bear, which lay by the door of the lodge, the hunter took his leave, bewailing bitterly at heart the loss of his friend and his bear.

He was scarcely out of sight when Manabozho sent the children to get red willow sticks. Of these he cut off as many pieces, of equal length, as would serve to invite his friends among the beasts and birds to a feast. A red stick was sent to each one, not forgetting the woodpecker and his family.

When they arrived they were astonished to see such an abundance of meat prepared for them at such a time of scarcity. Manabozho understood their glance, and was proud of a chance to make such a display.

"Akewazi," he said to the oldest of the party, "the weather is very cold, and the snow lasts a long time; we can kill nothing now but small squirrels, and they are all black; and I have sent for you to help me eat some of them."

The woodpecker was the first to try a mouthful of the bear's meat, but he had no sooner began to taste it than it changed into a dry powder, and set him coughing. It appeared as bitter as ashes.

The moose was affected in the same way, and it brought on such a dry cough as to shake every bone in his body.

One by one, each in turn joined the company of coughers, except Manabozho and his family, to whom the bear's meat proved very savory.

But the visitors had too high a sense of what was due to decorum and good manners to say any thing. The meat looked very fine, and being keenly set and strongly tempted by its promising look, they thought

they would try more of it. The more they ate the
faster they coughed, and the louder became the uproar, until Manabozho, exerting the magical gift
which he found he retained, changed them all into
squirrels ; and to this day the squirrel suffers from
the same dry cough which was brought on by attempting to sup off of Manabozho's ashen bear's
meat.

And ever after this transformation, when Manabozho lacked provisions for his family he would hunt
the squirrel, a supply of which never failed him, so
that he was always sure to have a number of his
friends present, in this shape, at the banquet.

The rock into which he changed the hunter, and
so became possessed of the bear, and thus laid the
foundations of his good fortune, ever after remained
by his lodge-door, and it was called the Game-Bag
of Manabozho, the Mischief-Maker.

XIX.

LEELINAU, THE LOST DAUGHTER,

L EELINAU was the favorite daughter of a hunter, who lived on the lake shore near the base of the lofty highlands, called Kaug Wudjoo.

From her earliest youth she was observed to be thoughtful and retiring. She passed much of her time in solitude, and seemed ever to prefer the companionship of her own shadow to the society of the lodge-circle.

Whenever she could leave her father's lodge she would fly to remote haunts and recesses in the woods, or sit in lonely reverie upon some high promontory of rock overlooking the lake. In such places she would often, with her face turned upward, linger long in contemplation of the air, as if she were invoking her guardian spirit, and beseeching him to lighten her sadness.

But amid all the leafy haunts, none drew her steps toward it so often as a forest of pines, on the open shore, called Manitowok, or the Sacred Wood. It was one of those hàllowed places which is the resort of the little wild men of the woods, and of the turtle spirits or fairies which delight in romantic scenes. Owing to this circumstance, its green retirement was seldom visited by Indians, who feared to fall under the influence of its mischievous inhabitants.

And whenever they were compelled by stress of weather to make a landing on this part of the coast, they never failed to leave an offering of tobacco, or some other token, to show that they desired to stand well with the proprietors of the fairy ground.

To this sacred spot Leelinau had made her way at an early age, gathering strange flowers and plants, which she would bring home to her parents, and relate to them all the haps and mishaps that had occurred in her rambles.

Although they discountenanced her frequent visits to the place, they were not able to restrain them, for she was of so gentle and delicate a temper that they feared to thwart her.

Her attachment to the fairy wood, therefore, grew with her years. If she wished to solicit her spirits to procure pleasant dreams, or any other maiden favor, Leelinau repaired to the Manitowok. If her father remained abroad in the hunt later than usual, and it was feared that he had been overwhelmed by the tempest, or had met with some other mischance, Leelinau offered up her prayers for safety at the Manitowok. It was there that she fasted, mused, and strolled.

She at length became so engrossed by the fairy pines that her parents began to suspect that some evil spirit had enticed her to its haunts, and had cast upon her a charm which she had not the power to resist.

This belief was confirmed when, one day, her mother, who had secretly followed her, overheard her murmuring to some unknown and invisible companion, appeals like these:

"Spirit of the dancing leaves!" whispered Leelinau, "hear a throbbing heart in its sadness. Spirit of the foaming stream! visit thou my nightly pillow, shedding over it silver dreams of mountain brook and pebbly rivulet. Spirit of the starry night! lead my foot-prints to the blushing mis-kodeed, or where the burning passion-flower shines with carmine hue. Spirit of the greenwood plume!" she concluded, turning with passionate gaze to the beautiful young pines which stood waving their green beauty over her head, "shed on me, on Leelinau the sad, thy leafy fragrance, such as spring unfolds from sweetest flowers, or hearts that to each other show their inmost grief. Spirits! hear, O hear a maiden's prayer!"

Day by day, these strange communings with unseen beings drew away the heart of Leelinau more and more from the simple duties of the lodge, and she walked among her people, melancholy and silent, like a spirit who had visited them from another land.

The pastimes which engaged the frolic moments of her young companions, passed by her as little trivial pageants in which she had no concern.

When the girls of the neighboring lodges assembled to play at the favorite female game of pappus-e-ko-waun, or the block and string, before the lodge-door, Leelinau would sit vacantly by, or enter so feebly into the spirit of the play as to show that it was irksome to her.

Again, in the evening, when the young people formed a ring around the lodge, and the piepeend-jigun, or leather and bone, passed rapidly from one to the other, she either handed it along without attempting to play, or if she took a part, it was with no effort to succeed.

The time of the corn-gathering had come, and the young people of the tribe were assembled in the field, busy in plucking the ripened maize. One of the girls, noted for her beauty, had found a red ear, and every one congratulated her that a brave admirer was on his way to her father's lodge. She blushed, and hiding the trophy in her bosom, she thanked the Good Spirit that it was a red ear, and not a crooked, that she had found.

Presently it chanced that one who was there among the young men, espied in the hands of Leelinau, who had plucked it indifferently, one of the crooked kind, and at once the word "Wa-ge-min !" was shouted aloud through the field, and the whole circle was set in a roar.

"The thief is in the corn-field !" exclaimed the young man, Iagoo by name, and famous in the tribe for his mirthful powers of story-telling ; " see you not the old man stooping as he enters the field ? See you not signs that he crouched as he crept in the dark ? Is it not plain by this mark on the stalk that he was heavily bent in his back ? Old man ! be nimble, or some one will take thee while thou art taking the ear."

These questions Iagoo accompanied with the action of one bowed with age stealthily entering the corn-field. He went on :

" See how he stoops as he breaks off the ear. Nushka ! He seems for a moment to tremble. Walker, be nimble ! Hooh ! It is plain the old man is the thief."

He turned suddenly where she sat in the circle, pensively regarding the crooked ear which she held in her hand, and exclaimed :

" Leelinau, the old man is thine !"

Laughter rung merrily through the corn-field, but Leelinau, casting down upon the ground the crooked ear of maize, walked pensively away.

The next morning the eldest son of a neighboring

chief called at her father's lodge He was quite advanced in years; but he enjoyed such renown in battle, and his name was so famous in the hunt, that
the parents accepted him as a suitor for their daughter. They hoped that his shining qualities would
draw brack the thoughts of Leelinau from that spirit-
land whither she seemed to have wholly directed her
affections.

It was this chief's son whom Iagoo had pictured
as the corn-taker, but, without objecting to his age, or
giving any other reason, Leelinau firmly declined his
proposals. The parents ascribed the young daughter's hesitancy to maiden fear, and paying no further
heed to her refusal, a day was fixed for the marriage-
visit to the lodge.

The young warrior came to the lodge-door, and
Leelinau refused to see him; informing her parents,
at the same time, that she would never consent to the
match.

It had been her custom to pass many of her hours
in her favorite place of retirement, under a broad-
topped young pine, whose leaves whispered in every
wind that blew; but most of all in that gentle murmur of the air at the evening hour, dear to lovers,
when the twilight steals on.

Thither she now repaired, and, while reclining pensively against the young pine-tree, she fancied that
she heard a voice addressing her. At first it was

scarcely more than a sigh; presently it grew more clear, and she heard it distinctly whisper—

"Maiden! think me not a tree; but thine own dear lover; fond to be with thee in my tall and blooming strength, with the bright green nodding plume that waves above thee. Thou art leaning on my breast, Leelinau; lean forever there and be at peace. Fly from men who are false and cruel, and quit the tumult of their dusty strife, for this quiet, lonely shade. Over thee I my arms will fling, fairer than the lodge's roof. I will breathe a perfume like that of flowers over thy happy evening rest. In my bark canoe I'll waft thee o'er the waters of the sky-blue lake. I will deck the folds of thy mantle with the sun's last rays. Come, and on the mountain free rove a fairy bright with me!"

Leelinau drunk in with eager ear these magical words. Her heart was fixed. No warrior's son should clasp her hand. She listened in the hope to hear the airy voice speak more; but it only repeated, "Again! again!" and entirely ceased.

On the eve of the day fixed for her marriage, Leelinau decked herself in her best garments. She arranged her hair according to the fashion of her tribe, and put on all of her maiden ornaments in beautiful array. With a smile, she presented herself before her parents.

"I am going," she said, "to meet my little lover,

the chieftain of the Green Plume, who is waiting for me at the Spirit Grove."

Her face was radiant with joy, and the parents, taking what she had said as her own fanciful way of expressing acquiescence in their plans, wished her good fortune in the happy meeting.

"I am going," she continued, addressing her mother as they left the lodge, "I am going from one who has watched my infancy and guarded my youth; who has given me medicine when I was sick, and prepared my food when I was well. I am going from a father who has ranged the forest to procure the choicest skins for my dress, and kept his lodge supplied with the best spoil of the chase. I am going from a lodge which has been my shelter from the storms of winter, and my shield from the heats of summer. Farewell, my parents, farewell!"

So saying, she sped faster than any could follow her to the margin of the fairy wood, and in a moment was lost to sight.

As she had often thus withdrawn herself from the lodge, the parents were not in fear, but confidently awaited her return. Hour chased hour, as the clouds of evening rolled up in the west; darkness came on, but no daughter returned. With torches they hastened to the wood, and although they lit up every dark recess and leafy gloom, their search was in vain. Leelinau was nowhere to be seen. They called aloud, in lament, upon her name, but she answered not.

Suns rose and set, but nevermore in their light did the bereaved parents eyes behold the lost form of their beloved child. Their daughter was lost indeed. Whither she had vanished no mortal tongue could tell; although it chanced that a company of fishermen, who were spearing fish near the Spirit Grove, descried something that seemed to resemble a female figure standing on the shore. As the evening was mild and the waters calm, they cautiously pulled their canoe toward land, but the slight ripple of their oars excited alarm. The figure fled in haste, but they could recognize in the shape and dress as she ascended the bank, the lost daughter, and they saw the green plumes of her fairy-lover waving over his forehead as he glided lightly through the forest of young pines.

XX.

THE WINTER-SPIRIT AND HIS VISITOR.

AN old man was sitting alone in his lodge by the side of a frozen stream. It was the close of winter, and his fire was almost out. He appeared very old and very desolate. His locks were white with age, and he trembled in every joint. Day after day passed in solitude, and he heard nothing but the sounds of the tempest, sweeping before it the new-fallen snow.

One day as his fire was just dying, a handsome young man approached and entered his dwelling. His cheeks were red with the blood of youth; his eyes sparkled with life, and a smile played upon his lips. He walked with a light and quick step. His fore-head was bound with a wreath of sweet grass, in place of the warrior's frontlet, and he carried a bunch of flowers in his hand

"Ah! my son," said the old man, "I am happy to see you. Come in. Come, tell me of your adventures, and what strange lands you have been to see.

Let us pass the night together. I will tell you of my prowess and exploits, and what I can perform. You shall do the same, and we will amuse ourselves."

He then drew from his sack a curiously-wrought antique pipe, and having filled it with tobacco, rendered mild by an admixture of certain dried leaves, he handed it to his guest. When this ceremony was attended to, they began to speak.

"I blow my breath," said the old man, "and the streams stand still. The water becomes stiff and hard as clear stone."

"I breathe," said the young man, "and flowers spring up all over the plains."

"I shake my locks," retorted the old man, "and snow covers the land. The leaves fall from the trees at my command, and my breath blows them away. The birds rise from the water and fly to a distant land. The animals hide themselves from the glance of my eye, and the very ground where I walk becomes as hard as flint."

"I shake my ringlets," rejoined the young man, "and warm showers of soft rain fall upon the earth. The plants lift up their heads out of the ground like the eyes of children glistening with delight. My voice recalls the birds. The warmth of my breath unlocks the streams. Music fills the groves wherever I walk, and all nature welcomes my approach."

At length the sun begun to rise. A gentle warmth

came over the place. The tongue of the old man became silent. The robin and the blue-bird began to sing on the top of the lodge. The stream began to murmur by the door, and the fragrance of growing herbs and flowers came softly on the vernal breeze.

Daylight fully revealed to the young man the character of his entertainer. When he looked upon him he had the visage of Peboan, the icy old Winter-Spirit. Streams began to flow from his eyes. As the sun increased he grew less and less in stature, and presently he had melted completely away. Nothing remained on the place of his lodge-fire but the miskodeed, a small white flower with a pink border, which the young visitor, Seegwun, the Spirit of Spring, placed in the wreath upon his brow, as his first trophy in the North.

XXI.

THE FIRE-PLUME.

WASSAMO was living with his parents on the shore of a large bay, far out in the north-east.

One day, when the season had commenced for fish to be plenty, the mother of Wassamo said to him, "My son, I wish you would go to yonder point and see if you can not procure me some fish; and ask your cousin to accompany you."

He did so. They set out, and in the course of the afternoon they arrived at the fishing-ground.

The cousin, being the elder, attended to the nets, and they encamped near by, using the bark of the birch for a lodge to shelter them through the night.

They lit a fire, and while they sat conversing with each other, the moon arose. Not a breath of wind disturbed the smooth surface of the lake. Not a cloud was seen. Wassamo looked out on the water toward their nets, and he saw that the little black spots, which were no other than the floats, dotting the lake, had disappeared.

" Cousin," he said, "let us visit our nets; perhaps we are fortunate."

When they drew up the nets they were rejoiced to see the meshes shining white, all over, with the glittering prey. They landed in fine spirits, and put away their canoe in safety from the winds.

" Wassamo," said the cousin, " you cook that we may eat."

Wassamo set about the work at once, and soon had his great kettle swung upon its branch, while the cousin lay at his ease upon the other side of the fire.

" Cousin," said Wassamo, " tell me stories or sing me some love-songs."

The cousin obeyed, and sung his plaintive songs; or he would frequently break off in the midst of a mournful chant, and begin to recite a mirthful story, and then in the midst of Wassamo's laughter he would return to the plaintive ditty—just as it suited his fancy ; for the cousin was gay of spirit, and shifted his humor faster than the fleecy clouds that appeared and disappeared in the night-sky over their heads. In this changeful pastime the cousin ran his length, and then he fell away, murmuring parts of his song or story, into a silvery sleep; with the moon gliding through the branches and gilding his face.

Wassamo in the mean while had lost the sound of

his cousin's voice in the rich simmer of the kettle; and when its music pleased his ear the most, as announcing that the fish were handsomely cooked, he lifted the kettle from the fire. He spoke to his cousin, but he received no answer.

He went on with his housekeeping alone, and took the wooden ladle and skimmed the kettle neatly, for the fish were very plump and fat. Wassamo had a torch of twisted bark in one hand to give light, and when he came to take out the fish, there was no one to have charge of the torch.

The cousin was so happy in his sleep, with the silver moon kissing his cheeks, as though she were enamored of his fair looks, that Wassamo had not the heart to call him up.

Binding his girdle upon his brow, in this he thrust the torch, and went forward, with the light dancing through the green leaves at every turn of his head, to prepare the evening meal.

He again spoke to his cousin, but gently, to learn whether he was in truth asleep. The cousin murmured, but made no reply; and Wassamo stepped softly about with the dancing fire-plume lighting up the gloom of the forest at every turn he made.

Suddenly he heard a laugh. It was double, or the one must be the perfect echo of the other. To Wassamo there appeared to be two persons at no great distance.

"Cousin," said Wassamo, "some person is near us. I hear a laugh; awake and let us look out !"

The cousin made no answer.

Again Wassamo heard the laughter in mirthful repetition, like the ripple of the water-brook upon the shining pebbles of the stream. Peering out as far as the line of the torchlight pierced into the darkness, he beheld two beautiful young females smiling on him. Their countenances appeared to be perfectly white, like the fresh snow.

He crouched down and pushed his cousin, saying, in a low voice, "Awake! awake! here are two young women."

But he received no answer. His cousin seemed lost to all earthly sense and sound; for he lay unmoved, smiling, in the calm light of the moon. Wassamo started up alone, and glided toward the strange females.

As he approached them he was more and more enraptured with their beauty; but just as he was about to speak to them, he suddenly fell to the earth, and they all three vanished together. The moon shone where they had just stood, but she saw them not. A gentle sound of music and soft voices accompanied their vanishing, and this wakened the cousin.

As he opened his eyes, in a dreamy way, he saw the kettle near him. Some of the fish he observed were in the bowl. The fire flickered, and made light and shadow; but nowhere was Wassamo to be seen. He waited, and waited again, in the expectation that Wassamo would appear.

"Perhaps," thought the cousin, "he is gone out again to visit the nets."

He looked off that way, but the canoe still lay close by the rock at the shore. He searched and found his footsteps in the ashes, and out upon the green ground a little distance, and then they were utterly lost.

He was now greatly troubled in spirit, and he called aloud, "Netawis! cousin! cousin!" but there was no answer to his call. He called again in his sorrow, louder and louder, "Netawis! Netawis! cousin! cousin! whither are you gone?" But no answer came to his voice of wailing. He started for the edge of the woods, crying as he ran, "My cousin!" and "Oh, my cousin!"

Hither and thither through the forest he sped with all his fleetness of foot and quickness of spirit; and when at last he found that no voice would answer him, he burst into tears, and sobbed aloud.

He returned to the fire, and sat down. He mused upon the absence of Wassamo with a sorely-troubled heart. "He may have been playing me a trick," he thought; but it was full time that the trick should be at an end, and Wassamo returned not. The cousin cherished other hopes, but they all died away in the morning light, when he found himself alone by the hunting-fire,

"How shall I answer to his friends for Wassamo?" thought the cousin. "Although," he said to himself, "his parents are my kindred, and they are well assured that their son is my bosom-friend, will they receive that belief in the place of him who is lost. No, no; they will say that I have slain him, and they will require blood for blood. Oh! my cousin, whither are you gone?"

He would have rested to restore his mind to its peace, but he could not sleep; and, without further regard to net or canoe, he set off for the village, running all the way.

As they saw him approaching at such speed and alone, they said, "Some accident has happened."

When he had come into the village, he told them how Wassamo had disappeared. He stated all the circumstances. He kept nothing to himself. He declared all that he knew.

Some said, "He has killed him in the dark." Others said, "It is impossible; they were like brothers; they would have fallen for each other. It can not be."

At the cousin's request, many of the men visited the fish-fire. There were no marks of blood. No hasty steps were there to show that any conflict or struggle had occurred. Every leaf on every tree was in its place; and they saw, as the cousin had before, that the foot-prints of Wassamo stopped in the wood, as if he had gone no further upon the earth, but had ascended into the air.

They returned to the village, and no man was the wiser as to the strange and sudden vanishing of Wassamo. None ever looked to see him more; only the parents, who still hoped and awaited his return.

The spring, with all its blossoms and its delicate newness of life, came among them; the Indians assembled to celebrate their vernal feast from all the country round.

Among them came the sad cousin of Wassamo. He was pale and thin as the shadow of the shaft that flies. The pain of his mind had changed his features, and wherever he turned his eyes, they were dazzled with the sight of the red blood of his friend.

The parents of Wassamo, far gone in despair, and weary with watching for his return, now demanded the life of Netawis. The village was stirred to its very heart by their loud lamentings ; and, after a struggle of pity, they decided to give the young man's life to the parents. They said that they had waited long enough. A day was appointed on which the cousin was to yield his life for his friend's.

He was a brave youth, and they bound him only by his word to be ready at the appointed hour. He

said that he was not afraid to die; for he was innocent of the great wrong they laid to his charge.

A day or two before the time set to take his life,
he wandered sadly along the shore of the lake. He
looked at the glassy water, and more than once the
thought to end his griefs by casting himself in its
depths, came upon him with such sudden force that it
was only by severe self-control that he was able to
turn his steps in another direction. He reflected —
"They will say that I was guilty if I take my own
life. No. I will give them my blood for that of my
cousin."

He walked on, with slow steps, but he found no
comfort, turn where he would; the sweet songs of the
grove jarred upon his ear; the beauty of the blue sky
pained his sight; and the soft green earth, as he
trode upon it, seemed harsh to his foot, and sent a
pang through every nerve. "Oh, where is my cousin?" he kept saying to himself.

Meanwhile, when Wassamo fell senseless before
the two young women in the wood, he lost all knowledge of himself until he wakened in a distant scene.
He heard persons conversing. One spoke in a tone of
command, saying, "You foolish girls, is this the way
that you rove about at nights without our knowledge?
Put that person you have brought on that couch of
yours, and do not let him lie upon the ground."

Wassamo felt himself moved, he knew not how,

and placed upon a couch. Some time after, the spell seemed to be a little lightened, and on opening his eyes, he was surprised to find that he was lying in a spacious and shining lodge, extending as far as the eye could reach.

One spoke to him and said : " Stranger, awake, and take something wherewith to refresh yourself."

He obeyed the command and sat up. On either side of the lodge he beheld rows of people seated in orderly array. At a distance he could see two stately persons, who looked rather more in years than the others, and who appeared to exact obedience from all around them. One of them, whom he heard addressed as the Old Spirit-man, spoke to Wassamo. "My son," said he, "know it was those foolish girls who brought you hither. They saw you at the fishing-ground. When you attempted to approach them you fell senseless, and at the same moment they transported you to this place. We are under the earth. But be at ease. We will make your stay with us pleasant. I am the guardian Spirit of the Sand Mountains. They are my charge. I pile them up, and blow them about, and do whatever I will with them. It keeps me very busy, but I am hale for my age, and I love to be employed. I have often wished to get one of your race to marry among us. If you can make up your mind to remain, I will give you one of my daughters—the one who smiled on you first, the night you were brought away from your parents and friends."

Wassamo dropped his head and made no answer. The thought that he should behold his kindred no more, made him sad.

He was silent, and the Old Spirit continued: "Your wants will all be supplied; but you must be careful not to stray far from the lodge. I am afraid of that Spirit who rules all islands lying in the lakes. He is my bitter enemy, for I have refused him my daughter in marriage; and when he learns that you are a member of my family, he will seek to harm you. There is my daughter," added the Old Spirit, pointing toward her. "Take her. She shall be your wife."

Forthwith Wassamo and the Old Spirit's daughter sat near each other in the lodge, and they were man and wife.

One evening the Old Spirit came in after a busy day's work out among the sand-hills, in the course of which he had blown them all out of shape with great gusts of wind, and strewn them about in a thousand directions, and brought them back and piled them up in all sorts of misshapen heaps.

At the close of this busy day, when the Old Spirit came in very much out of breath, he said to Wassamo, "Son-in-law, I am in want of tobacco. None grows about this dry place of mine. You shall return to your people and procure me a supply. It is seldom that the few who pass these sand-hills offer me a piece of tobacco,–it is a rare plant in these parts,–but when they do, it immediately comes to me. Just so," he added, putting his hand out of the side of the lodge and drawing in several pieces of tobacco which some one passing at that moment offered as a fee to the Old Spirit, to keep the sand-hills from blowing about till they had got by.

Other gifts beside tobacco came in the same way to the side of the lodge—sometimes a whole bear, then a wampum-robe, then a string of birds—and the Sand-Spirits alogether led an easy life; for they were not at the trouble to hunt or clothe themselves; and whenever the housekeeping began to fall short, nothing would happen but a wonderful storm of dust, all the sand-hills being straightway put in an uproar, and the contributions would at once begin to pour in at the side windows of the lodge, till all their wants were supplied.

After Wassamo had been among these curious people several months, the old Sand-Spirit said to him, "Son-in-law, you must not be surprised at what you will see next; for since you have been with us you have never known us to go to sleep. It has been summer when the sun never sets here where we live. But now, what you call winter, is coming on. You will soon see us lie down, and we shall not rise again till the spring. Take my advice. Do not leave the lodge. I have sure knowledge that that knavish Island Spirit is on the prowl, and as he has command of a particular kind of storm, which comes from the south-west, he only waits his opportunity to catch you abroad and do you a mischief. Try and amuse yourself. That cupboard," pointing to a corner of the lodge, "is never empty; for it is there that all the offerings are handed in while we are asleep. It is never empty, and—" But ere the old Sand-Spirit could utter another word, a loud rattling of thunder was heard, and instantly, not only the Old Spirit but every one of his family, vanished out of sight.

When the storm had passed by, they all reappeared in the lodge. This sudden vanishing and reappearance occurred at every tempest.

"You are surprised," said the Old Spirit, "to see us disappear when it thunders. The reason is this: that noise which you fancy is thunder, is our enemy the Island Spirit hallooing on his way home from the hunt. We get out of sight that we may escape the necessity of asking him to come in and share our evening meal. We are not afraid of him, not in the least."

Just then it chanced to thunder again, and Wassamo observed that his father-in-law made extraordinary dispatch to conceal himself, although no stranger, at all resembling in any way the Island Spirit, was in view.

Shortly after this the season of sleep began, and one by one they laid themselves down to the long slumber.

The Old Spirit was the last to drop away; and, before he yielded, he went forth and had his last sport with the sand-hills, and he so tossed and vexed the poor hills, and scattered them to and fro, and whirled them up in the air, and far over the land, that it was days and days before they got back to any thing like their natural shape.

While his relations were enjoying this long sleep, Wassamo amused himself as best he could. The cupboard never failed him once; for visit it when he would, he always found a fresh supply of game, and every other dainty which his heart desired.

But his chief pastime was to listen to the voices of the travelers who passed by the window at the side of the lodge where they made their requests for comfortable weather and an easy journey.

These were often mingled with loud complainings, such as "Ho! how the sand jumps about!" "Take away that hill!" "I am lost!" "Old Sand-Spirit, where are you? help this way!" and the like, which indicated that such as were journeying through the hills had their own troubles to encounter.

As the spring-light of the first day of spring shone into the lodge, the whole family arose and went about the affairs of the day as though they had been slumbering only for a single night. The rest of the Old Spirit seemed to have done him much good, for he was very cheerful; and, first putting his head forth from the window for a puff at a sand-hill, which was his prime luxury in a morning, he said to Wassamo, " Son-in-law, you have been very patient with our long absence from your company, and you shall be rewarded. In a few days you may start with your wife to visit your relations. You can be absent one year, but at the end of that time you must return. When you get to your home-village, you must first go in alone. Leave your wife at a short distance from the lodge, and when you are welcome, then send for her. When there, do not be surprised that she disappears whenever you hear it thunder." He added, with a sly look, " That old Island Spirit has a brother down in that part of the country. You will prosper in all things, for my daughter is very diligent. All the time that you pass in sleep, she will be at work. The distance is short to your village. A path leads directly to it, and when you get there do not forget my wants as I stated to you before."

Wassamo promised obedience to these directions, and, at the appointed time, set out in company with his wife. They traveled on a pleasant course, his wife leading the way, until they reached a rising ground.

At the highest point of this ground, she said, " We will soon get to your country."

It suddenly became broad day, as they came upon a high bank; they passed, unwet, for a short distance under the lake, and presently emerged from the water at the sand-banks, just off the shore where Wassamo had set his nets on the night when he had been borne away by the two strange females.

He now left his wife sheltered in a neighboring wood, while he advanced toward the village alone.

Musing sadly, and from time to time breaking forth in mournful cries, as he walked the shore, it was his cousin that Wassamo beheld as he turned the first point of land by the lake.

With the speed of lightning the cousin rushed forward. "Netawis! Netawis!" he cried, "is it indeed you? Whence have you come, oh, my cousin?"

They fell upon each other's necks, and wept aloud. And then, without further delay or question, the cousin ran off with breathless dispatch to the village. He seemed like a shadow upon the open ground, he sped so fast.

He entered the lodge where sat the mother of Wassamo in mourning for her son. "Hear me," said the cousin. "I have seen him whom you accuse me of having killed. He will be here even while we speak."

He had scarcely uttered these words when the whole village was astir in an instant. All ran out and strained their eyes to catch the first view of him whom they had thought dead. And when Wassamo came forward, they at first fell from him as though he had been in truth one returned from the Spirit-land. He entered the lodge of his parents. They saw that it was Wassamo, living, breathing and as they had ever known him. And joy lit up the lodge-circle as though a new fire had been kindled in the eyes of his friends and kinsfolk.

He related all that had happened to him from the moment of his leaving the temporary night-lodge with the flame on his head. He told them of the strange land in which he had sojourned during his absence. He added to his mother, apart from the company, that he was married, and that he had left his wife at a short distance from the village.

She went out immediately in search of her; they soon found her in the wood, and all the women in the village conducted her in honor to the lodge of her new relations. The Indian people were astonished at her beauty, at the whiteness of her skin, and still more, that she was able to talk with them in their own language.

The village was happy, and the feast went on as long as the supply held out. All were delighted to make the acquaintance of the old Sand-Spirit's daughter; and as they had heard that he was a magician and guardian of great power, the tobacco which he had sent for by his son-in-law, came in, in great abundance, with every visitor.

The summer and fall which Wassamo thus passed with his parents and the people of his tribe were prosperous with all the country.

The cousin of Wassamo recovered heart, and sang once more his sad or mirthful chants, just as the humor was upon him; but he kept close by Wassamo, and watched him in all his movements. He made it a point to ask many questions of the country he came from; some of which his cousin replied to, but others were left entirely in the dark.

At every thunder-storm, as the old Sand-Spirit had foreboded, the wife of Wassamo disappeared, much to the astonishment of her Indian company, and, to their greater wonder, she was never idle, night nor day.

When the winter came on, Wassamo prepared for her a comfortable lodge, to which she withdrew for her long sleep; and he gave notice to his friends that they must not disturb her, as she would not be with them again until the spring returned.

Before lying down, she said to her husband, "No one but yourself must pass on this side of the lodge."

The winter passed away with snows, and sports and stories in the lodge; and when the sap of the maple began to flow, the wife of Wassamo wakened, and she immediately set about work as before. She helped at the maple-trees with the others; and, as if luck were in her presence, the sugar-harvest was greater than had been ever known in all that region.

The gifts of tobacco, after this, came in even more freely than they had at first; and as each brought his bundle to the lodge of Wassamo, he asked for the usual length of life, for success as a hunter, and for a plentiful supply of food. They particularly desired that the sand-hills might be kept quiet, so that their lands might be moist, and their eyes clear of dust to sight the game.

Wassamo replied that he would mention each of their requests to his father-in-law.

The tobacco was stored in sacks, and on the outside of the skins, that there might be no mistake as to their wants, each one who had given tobacco had painted and marked in distinct characters the totem or family emblem of his family and tribe. These the old Sand-Spirit could read at his leisure, and do what he thought best for each of his various petitioners.

When the time for his return arrived, Wassamo warned his people that they should not follow him nor attempt to take note how he disappeared. He then took the moose-skin sacks filled with tobacco, and bade farewell to all but Netawis. He insisted on the privilege of attending Wassamo and his wife for a distance, and when they reached the sand-banks he expressed the strongest wish to proceed with them or their journey. Wassamo told him that it could not be; that only spirits could exert the necessary power, and that there were no such spirits at hand.

They then took an affectionate leave of each other, Wassamo enjoining it upon his cousin, at risk of his life, to not look back when he had once started to return.

The cousin, sore at heart, but constrained to obey, parted from them, and as he walked sadly away, he heard a gliding noise as of the sound of waters that were cleaved.

He returned home, and told his friends that Wassamo and his wife had disappeard, but that he knew not how. No one doubted his word in any thing now.

Wassamo with his wife soon reached their home at the hills. The old Sand-Spirit was in excellent health, and delighted to see them. He hailed their return with open arms; and he opened his arms so very wide, that when he closed them he not only embraced Wassamo and his wife, but all of the tobacco-sacks which they had brought with them.

The requests of the Indian people were made known to him; he replied that he would attend to all, but that he must first invite his friends to smoke with him. Accordingly he at once dispatched his pipe-bearer and confidential aid to summon various Spirits of his acquaintance, and set the time for them to come.

Meanwhile he had a word of advice for his son-in-law Wassamo. " My son," said he, " some of these Manitos that I have asked to come here are of a very wicked temper, and I warn you especially of that Island Spirit who wished to marry my daughter. He is a very bad-hearted Monedo, and would like to do you harm. Some of the company you will, however, find to be very friendly. A caution for you. When they come in, do you sit close by your wife; if you do not, you will be lost. She only can save you; for those who are expected to come are so powerful that they will otherwise draw you from your seat, and toss you out of the lodge as though you were a feather. You have only to observe my words and all will be well."

Wassamo took heed to what the Old Spirit said, and answered that he would obey.

About mid-day the company began to assemble; and such a company Wassamo had never looked on before. There were Spirits from all parts of the country; such strange-looking persons, and in dresses so wild and outlandish ! One entered who smiled on him This, Wassamo was informed, was a Spirit who had charge of the affairs of a tribe in the North, and he was as pleasant and cheery a Spirit as one would wish to see. Soon after, Wassamo heard a great rumbling and roaring, as of waters tumbling over rocks; and presently, with a vast bluster, and fairly shaking the lodge with his deep-throated hail of welcome to the old Sand-Spirit, in rolled another, who was the Guardian Spirit and special director of a great cataract or water-fall not far off.

Then came with crashing steps the owner of several whirlwinds, which were in the habit of raging about in the neighboring country. And following this one, glided in a sweet-spoken, gentle-faced little Spirit, who was understood to represent a summer-gale that was accustomed to blow, toward evening, in at the lodge-doors, and to be particularly well disposed toward young lovers.

The last to appear was a great rocky-headed fellow; and he was twice as stony in his manners; and swaggered and strided in, and raised such a commotion with his great green blanket when he shook it, that Wassamo was nearly taken off his feet; and it was only by main force that he was able to cling by his wife. This, which was the last to enter, was that wicked Island Spirit, who looked grim enough at Wassamo's wife, who had rejected him, as he passed in.

Soon after, the old Sand-Spirit, who was a great speech-maker, arose and addressed the assembly.

"Brothers," he said, "I have invited you to partake with me of the offerings made by the mortals on earth, which have been brought by our relation," pointing to Wassamo. "Brothers, you see their wishes and desires plainly set forth here," laying his hand upon the figured moose-skins. " The offering is worthy of our consideration. Brothers, I see nothing on my part to hinder our granting their requests; they do not appear to be unreasonable. Brothers, the offer is gratifying. It is tobacco—an article which we have lacked until we scarcely knew how to use our pipes. Shall we grant their requests? One thing more I would say. Brothers, it is this: There is my son-in law; he is mortal. I wish to detain him with me, and it is with us jointly to make him one of us."

" Hoke! hoke!" ran through the whole company of Spirits, and " Hoke! hoke!" they cried again. And it was understood that the petitioners were to have all they asked, and that Wassamo was thenceforward fairly accepted as a member of the great family of Spirits.

As a wedding-gift, the Old Spirit asked his son-in-law to make one request, which should be promptly granted.

" Let there be no sand-squalls among my father's people for three months to come," said Wassamo.

" So shall it be," answered the old Sand-Spirit.

The tobacco was now divided in equal shares among the company. They filled their pipes—and huge pipes they were—and such clouds they blew, that they rushed forth out of the lodge and brought on night, in all the country round about, several hours before its time.

After a while passed in silence, the Spirits rose up, and bearing off their tobacco-sacks, they went smoking through the country, and losing themselves in their own fog, till a late hour in the morning, when all of their pipes being burned out, each departed on his own business.

The very next day the old Sand-Spirit, who was very much pleased with the turn affairs had taken at his entertainment, addressed Wassamo : " Son-in-law, I have made up my mind to allow you another holiday as an acknowledgment of the handsome manner in which you acquitted yourself of your embassy. You may visit your parents and relatives once more, to tell them that their wishes are granted, and to take your leave of them forever. You can never, after, visit them again."

Wassamo at once set out, reached his people, and was heartily welcomed.

They asked for his wife, and Wassamo informed them that she had tarried at home to look after a son, a fine little Sand-Spirit, who had been born to them since his return.

Having delivered all of his messages and passed a happy time, Wassamo said, " I must now bid you all farewell forever."

His parents and friends raised their voices in loud

lamentation; they clung to him, and as a specia favor, which he could now grant, being himself a spirit, he allowed them to accompany him to the sand-banks.

They all seated themselves to watch his last farewell. The day was mild; the sky clear, not a cloud appearing to dim the heavens, nor a breath of wind to ruffle the tranquil waters. A perfect silence fell upon the company. They gazed with eager eyes fastened on Wassamo, as he waded out into the water, waving his hands. They saw him descend, more and more, into the depths. They beheld the waves close over his head, and a loud and piercing wail went up which rent the sky.

They looked again; a red flame, as if the sun had glanced on a billow, lighted the spot for an instant; but the Feather of Flames, Wassamo of the Fire-Plume, had disappeared from home and kindred, **and** the familiar paths of his youth, forever.

XXII.

WEENDIGOES AND THE BONE-DWARF.

IN a lonely forest, there once lived a man and his wife, who had a son. The father went forth every day, according to the custom of the Indians, to hunt for food to supply his family.

One day, while he was absent, his wife, on going out of the lodge, looked toward the lake that was near, and she saw a very large man walking on the water, and coming fast toward the lodge. He was already so near that she could not, if she had wished to, escape by flight. She thought to herself, " What shall I say to the monster ?"

As he advanced rapidly, she ran in, and taking the hand of her son, a boy of three or four years old, she led him out. Speaking very loud, " See, my son," she said, " your grandfather;" and then added, in a tone of appeal and supplication, " he will have pity on us."

The giant approached and said, with a loud ha! ha! " Yes, my son;" and added, addressing the woman, " Have you any thing to eat ?"

By good luck the lodge was well supplied with meats of various kinds; the woman thought to please him by handing him these, which were savory and carefully prepared. But he pushed them away in disgust, saying, " I smell fire;" and, not waiting to be invited, he seized upon the carcass of a deer which lay by the door, and dispatched it almost without stopping to take breath.

When the hunter came home he was surprised to see the monster, he was so very frightful. He had again brought a deer, which he had no sooner put down than the cannibal seized it, tore it in pieces, and devoured it as though he had been fasting for a week. The hunter looked on in fear and astonishment, and in a whisper he told his wife that he was afraid for their lives, as this monster was one whom Indians call Weendigoes. He did not even dare to speak to him, nor did the cannibal say a word, but as soon as he had finished his meal, he stretched himself down and fell asleep.

In the evening the Weendigo told the people that he should go out a hunting; and he strided away toward the North. Toward morning he returned, all besmeared with blood, but he did not make known where he had been nor of what kind of game he had been in quest; although the hunter and his wife had dreadful suspicions of the sport in which he had been engaged. Withal his hunger did not seem to be

13

staid, for he took up the deer which the hunter had brought in, and devoured it eagerly, leaving the family to make their meal of the dried meats which had been reserved in the lodge.

In this manner the Weendigo and the hunter's family lived for some time, and it surprised them that the monster never attempted their lives; although he never slept at night, but always went out and returned, by the break of day, stained with blood, and looking very wild and famished. When there was no deer to be had wherewith to finish his repast, he said nothing. In truth he was always still and gloomy, and he seldom spoke to any of them; when he did, his discourse was chiefly addressed to the boy.

One evening, after he had thus sojourned with them for many weeks, he informed the hunter that the time had now arrived for him to take his leave, but that before doing so, he would give him a charm that would bring good luck to his lodge. He presented to him two arrows, and thanking the hunter and his wife for their kindness, the Weendigo departed, saying, as he left them, that he had all the world to travel over.

The hunter and his wife were happy when he was gone, for they had looked every moment to have been devoured by him. He tried the arrows, and they never failed to bring down whatever they were aimed at.

They had lived on, prosperous and contented, for a year, when, one day, the hunter being absent, his wife on going out of the lodge, saw something like a black cloud approaching.

She looked until it came near, when she perceived that it was another Weendigo or Giant Cannibal. Remembering the good conduct of the other, she had no fear of this one, and asked him to look into the lodge.

He did so ; and finding after he had glared around, that there was no food at hand, he grew very wroth, and, being sorely disappointed, he took the lodge and threw it to the winds. He seemed hardly at first to notice the woman in his anger; but presently he cast a fierce glance upon her, and seizing her by the waist, in spite of her cries and entreaties, he bore her off. To the little son, who ran to and fro lamenting, he paid no heed.

At night-fall, when the hunter returned from the forest, he was amazed. His lodge was gone, and he saw his son sitting near the spot where it had stood, shedding tears. The son pointed in the direction the Weendigo had taken, and as the father hurried along he found the remains of his wife strewn upon the ground.

The hunter blackened his face, and vowed in his heart that he would have revenge. He built another lodge, and gathering together the bones of his wife, he placed them in the hollow part of a dry tree.

He left his boy to take care of the lodge while he was absent, hunting and roaming about from place to place, striving to forget his misfortune, and searching for the wicked Weendigo.

He had been gone but a little while one morning, when his son shot his arrows out through the top of the lodge, and running out to look for them, he could find them nowhere. The boy had been trying his luck, and he was puzzled that he had shot his shafts entirely out of sight.

His father made him more arrows, and when he was again left alone, he shot one of them out; but although he looked as sharply as he could toward the spot where it fell, and ran thither at once, he could not find it.

He shot another, which was lost in the same way; and returning to the lodge to replenish his quiver, he happened to espy one of the lucky arrows, which the first Weendigo had given to his father, hanging upon the side of the lodge. He reached up, and having secured it, he shot it out at the opening, and immediately running out to find where it fell, he was surprised to see a beautiful boy just in the act of taking it up, and hurrying away with it to a large tree, where he disappeared.

The hunter's son followed, and having come to

the tree, he beheld the face of the boy looking out through an opening in the hollow part.

"Ha! ha!" he said, "my friend, come out and play with me;" and he urged the boy till he consented. They played and shot their arrows by turns.

Suddenly the young boy said, "Your father is coming. We must stop. Promise me that you will not tell him."

The hunter's son promised, and the other disappeared in the tree.

When the hunter returned from the chase, his son sat demurely by the fire. In the course of the evening he asked his father to make him a new bow; and when he was questioned as to the use he could find for two bows, he answered that one might break or get lost.

The father pleased at his son's diligence in the practice of the bow, made him the two weapons; and the next day, as soon as his father had gone away, the boy ran to the hollow tree, and invited his little friend to come out and play; at the same time presenting to him the new bow. They went and played in the lodge together, and in their sport they raised the ashes all over it.

Suddenly again the youngest said, "Your father is coming, I must leave."

He again exacted a promise of secresy, and went

back to his tree. The eldest took his seat near the fire.

When the hunter came in he was surprised to see the ashes scattered about. " Why, my son," he said, " you must have played very hard to day to raise such a dust all alone."

" Yes," the boy answered, " I was very lonesome, and I ran round and round—that is the cause of it."

The next day the hunter made ready for the chase as usual. The boy said, " Father, try and hunt all day, and see what you can kill."

He had no sooner set out than the boy called his friend, and they played and chased each other round the lodge. They had great delight in each other's company, and made merry by the hour. The hunter was again returning, and came to a rising ground, which caught the winds as they passed, and he heard his son laughing and making a noise, but the sounds as they reached him on the hill-top, seemed as if they arose from two persons playing.

At the same time the younger boy stopped, and after saying " Your father is coming," he stole away, under cover of the high grass, to his hollow tree, which was not far off.

The hunter, on entering, found his son sitting by the fire, very quiet and unconcerned, although he saw that all the articles of the lodge were lying thrown about in all directions.

Why, my son," he said " you must play very hard every day; and what is it that you do, all alone, to throw the lodge in such confusion ?"

The boy again had his excuse. " Father," he answered, " I play in this manner : I chase and drag my blanket around the lodge, and that is the reason you see the ashes spread about."

The hunter was not satisfied until his son had shown him how he played with the blanket, which he did so adroitly as to set his father laughing, and at last drive him out of the lodge with the great clouds of ashes that he raised.

The next morning the boy renewed his request that his father should be absent all day, and see if he could not kill two deer. The hunter thought this a strange desire on the part of his son, but as he had always humored the boy, he went into the forest as usual, bent on accomplishing his wish, if he could.

As soon as he was out of sight, his son hastened to his young companion at the tree, and they continued their sports.

The father on nearing his home in the evening, as he reached the rising ground, again heard the sounds of play and laughter; and as the wind brought them straight to his ear, he was now certain that there were two voices.

The boy from the tree had no more than time to escape, when the hunter entered, and found his son, sitting as usual, near the fire. When he cast his eyes around, he saw that the lodge was in greater confusion than before. "My son," he said, "you must be very foolish when alone to play so. But, tell me, my son; I heard two voices, I am sure;" and he looked closely on the prints of the footsteps in the ashes. "True," he continued, "here is the print of a foot which is smaller than my son's;" and he was now satisfied that his suspicions were well founded, and that some very young person had been the companion of his son.

The boy could not now refuse to tell his father what had happened.

"Father," he said, "I found a boy in the hollow of that tree, near the lodge, where you placed my mother's bones."

Strange thoughts came over the mind of the hunter; did his wife live again in this beautiful child?

Fearful of disturbing the dead, he did not dare to visit the place where he had deposited her remains.

He, however, engaged his son to entice the boy to a dead tree, by the edge of a wood, where they could kill many flying-squirrels by setting it on fire. He said that he would conceal himself near by, and take the boy.

The next day the hunter accordingly went into the woods, and his son, calling the boy from the tree, urged him to go with him to kill the squirrels. The boy objected that his father was near, but he was at length prevailed on to go, and after they had firea the tree, and while they were busy killing or taking the squirrels, the hunter suddenly made his appearance, and clasped the strange boy in his arms. He cried out, " Kago, kago, don't, don't. You will tear my clothes !" for he was clad in a fine apparel, which shone as if it had been made of a beautiful transparent skin. The father reassured him by every means in his power.

By constant kindness and gentle words the boy was reconciled to remain with them; but chiefly by the presence of his young friend, the hunter's son, to whom he was fondly attached. The children were never parted from each other; and when the hunter looked upon the strange boy, he seemed to see living in him the better spirit of his lost wife. He was thankful to the Great Spirit for this act of goodness, and in his heart he felt assured that in time the boy would show great virtue, and in some way avenge him on the wicked Weendigo who had destroyed the companion of his lodge.

The hunter grew at ease in his spirit, and gave all of the time he could spare from the chase to the society of the two children ; but, what affected him the most, both of his sons, although they were well-formed and beautiful, grew no more in stature, but remained children still. Every day they resembled each other more and more, and they never ceased to

13*

sport and divert themselves in the innocent ways of childhood.

One day the hunter had gone abroad with his bow and arrows, leaving, at the request of the strange boy, one of the two shafts which the friendly Weendigo had given to him, behind in the lodge.

When he returned, what were his surprise and joy to see stretched dead by his lodge-door, the black giant who had slain his wife. He had been stricken down by the magic shaft in the hands of the little stranger from the tree; and ever after the boy, or the Bone-Dwarf as he was called, was the guardian and good genius of the lodge, and no evil spirit, giant, or Weendigo, dared approach it to mar their peace.

XXIII.

THE BIRD LOVER.

IN a region of country where the forest and the prairie strived which should be the most beautiful—the open plain, with its free sunshine and winds and flowers, or the close wood, with its delicious twilight-walks and enamored haunts—there lived a wicked manito in the disguise of an old Indian.

Although the country furnished an abundance of game, and whatever else a good heart could wish for, it was the study of this wicked genius to destroy such as fell into his hands. He made use of all his arts to decoy men into his power, for the purpose of killing them. The country had been once thickly peopled, but this Mudjee Monedo had so thinned it by his cruel practices, that he now lived almost solitary in the wilderness.

The secret of his success lay in his great speed. He had the power to assume the shape of any four-footed creature, and it was his custom to challenge such as he sought to destroy, to run with him. He had a beaten path on which he ran, leading around a large lake, and he always ran around this circle so that the starting and the winning-post was the same. Whoever failed as every one had, yielded up his life at this post; and although he ran every day, no man was ever known to beat this evil genius; for whenever he was pressed hard, he changed himself into a fox, wolf, deer, or other swift-footed animal, and was thus able to leave his competitor behind.

The whole country was in dread of this same Mudjee Monedo, and yet the young men were constantly running with him; for if they refused, he called them cowards, which was a reproach they could not bear. They would rather die than be called cowards.

To keep up his sport, the manito made light of these deadly foot-matches, and instead of assuming a braggart air, and going about in a boastful way, with the blood of such as he had overcome, upon his hands, he adopted very pleasing manners, and visited the lodges around the country as any other sweet-tempered and harmless old Indian might.

His secret object in these friendly visits was to learn whether the young boys were getting old enough to run with him; he kept a very sharp eye upon their growth, and the day he thought them ready, he did not fail to challenge them to a trial on his racing-ground.

There was not a family in all that beautiful region

which had not in this way been visited and thinned
out; and the manito had quite naturally come to be
held in abhorrence by all the Indian mothers in the
country.

It happened that there lived near him a poor
widow woman, whose husband and seven sons he had
made way with; and she was now living with an only
daughter, and a son of ten or twelve years old.

This widow was very poor and feeble, and she suffered so much for lack of food and other comforts of
the lodge, that she would have been glad to die, but for
her daughter and her little son. The Mudjee Monedo
had already visited her lodge to observe whether the
boy was sufficiently grown to be challenged to the
race; and so crafty in his approaches and so soft in
his manners was the monedo, that the mother feared
that he would yet decoy the son and make way with
him as he had done with his father and his seven
brothers, in spite of all her struggles to save him.

And yet she strove with all her might to strengthen
her son in every good course. She taught him, as best
she could, what was becoming for the wise hunter
and the brave warrior. She remembered and set before him all that she could recall of the skill and the
craft of his father and his brothers who were lost.

The widow woman also instructed her daughter in
whatever could make her useful as a wife; and in the
leisure-time of the lodge, she gave her lessons in the

art of working with the quills of porcupine, and
bestowed on her such other accomplishments as
should make her an ornament and a blessing to her
husband's household.   The daughter, Minda by
name, was kind and obedient to her mother, and
never failed in her duty.   Their lodge stood high
up on the banks of a lake, which gave them a wide
prospect of country, embellished with groves and
open fields, which waved with the blue light of their
long grass, and made, at all hours of sun and moon,
a cheerful scene to look upon.

Across this beautiful prairie, Minda had one morning made her way to gather dry limbs for their fire;
for she disdained no labor of the lodge.   And while
enjoying the sweetness of the air and the green
beauty of the woods, she strolled far away.

She had come to a bank, painted with flowers of
every hue, and was reclining on its fragrant couch,
when a bird, of red and deep-blue plumage softly
blended, alighted on a branch near by, and began to
pour forth its carol.   It was a bird of strange character, such as she had never before seen.   Its first
note was so delicious to the ear of Minda, and it so
pierced to her young heart, that she listened as she
had never before to any mortal or heavenly sound.   It
seemed like the human voice, forbidden to speak, and
uttering its language through this wild wood-chant
with a mournful melody, as if it bewailed the lack of

the power or the right to make itself more plainly intelligible.

The voice of the bird rose and fell, and circled round and round, but whithersoever floated or spread out its notes, they seemed ever to have their center where Minda sat; and she looked with sad eyes into the sad eyes of the mournful bird, that sat in his red and deep-blue plumage just opposite to the flowery bank.

The poor bird strove more and more with his voice, and seemed ever more and more anxiously to address his notes of lament to Minda's ear, till at last she could not refrain from saying, " What aileth thee, sad bird ?"

As if he had but waited to be spoken to, the bird left his branch, and alighting upon the bank, smiled on Minda, and, shaking his shining plumage, answered:

" I am bound in this condition until a maiden shall accept me in marriage. I have wandered these groves and sung to many and many of the Indian girls, but none ever heeded my voice till you. Will you be mine?" he added, and poured forth a flood of melody which sparkled and spread itself with its sweet murmurs over all the scene, and fairly entranced the young Minda, who sat silent, as if she feared to break the charm by speech.

The bird, approaching nearer, asked her, if she loved him, to get her mother's consent to their mar-

riage. " I shall be free then," said the bird, " and
you shall know me as I am."

Minda lingered, and listened to the sweet voice of
the bird in its own forest notes, or filling each pause
with gentle human discourse; questioning her as to
her home, her family, and the little incidents of her
daily life.

She returned to the lodge later than usual, but she
was too timid to speak to her mother of that which the
bird had charged her. She returned again and again
to the fragrant haunt in the wood; and every day she
listened to the song and the discourse of her bird admirer with more pleasure, and he every day besought
her to speak to her mother of the marriage. This
she could not, however, muster heart and courage to
do.

At last the widow began herself to have a suspicion that her daughter's heart was in the wood, from
her long delays in returning, and the little success
she had in gathering the fire-branches for which she
went in search.

In answer to her mother's questions, Minda revealed the truth, and made known her lover's request. The mother, considering the lonely and destitute condition of her little household, gave her consent.

The daughter, with light steps, hastened with the
news to the wood. The bird lover of course heard

it with delight, and fluttered through the air in happy circles, and poured forth a song of joy which thrilled Minda to the heart.

He said that he would come to the lodge at sunset, and immediately took wing, while Minda hung fondly upon his flight, till he was lost far away in the blue sky.

With the twilight the bird lover, whose name was Monedowa, appeared at the door of the lodge, as a hunter, with a red plume and a mantle of blue upon his shoulders.

He addressed the widow as his friend, and she directed him to sit down beside her daughter, and they were regarded as man and wife.

Early on the following morning, he asked for the bow and arrows of those who had been slain by the wicked manito, and went out a-hunting. As soon as he had got out of sight of the lodge, he changed himself into the wood-bird, as he had been before his marriage, and took his flight through the air.

Although game was scarce in the neighborhood of the widow's lodge, Monedowa returned at evening, in his character of a hunter, with two deer. This was his daily practice, and the widow's family never more lacked for food.

It was noticed, however, that Monedowa himself ate but little, and that of a peculiar kind of meat, flavored with berries, which, with other circumstances, convinced them that he was not as the Indian people around him.

In a few days his mother-in-law told him that the manito would come to pay them a visit, to see how the young man, her son, prospered.

Monedowa answered that he should on that day be absent. When the time arrived, he flew upon a tall tree, overlooking the lodge, and took his station there as the wicked manito passed in.

The mudjee monedo cast sharp glances at the scaffolds so well laden with meat, and as soon as he had entered, he said, " Why, who is it that is furnishing you with meat so plentifully?"

" No one," she answered, " but my son; he is just beginning to kill deer."

" No, no," he retorted; " some one is living with you."

" Kaween, no indeed," replied the widow; " you are only making sport of my hapless condition. Who do you think would come and trouble themselves about me?"

" Very well," answered the manito, " I will go; but on such a day I will again visit you, and see who it is that furnishes the meat, and whether it is your son or not."

He had no sooner left the lodge and got out of sight, than the son-in-law made his appearance with two more deer. On being made acquainted with the conduct of the manito, "Very well," he said, "I will be at home the next time, to see him."

Both the mother and the wife urged Monedowa to be aware of the manito. They made known to him all of his cruel courses, and assured him that no man could escape from his power.

"No matter," said Monedowa; "if he invites me to the race-ground, I will not be backward. What follows, may teach him, my mother, to show pity on the vanquished, and not to trample on the widow and those who are without fathers."

When the day of the visit of the manito arrived, Monedowa told his wife to prepare certain pieces of meat, which he pointed out to her, together with two or three buds of the birch-tree, which he requested her to put in the pot. He directed also that the manito should be hospitably received, as if he had been just the kind-hearted old Indian he professed to be. Monedowa then dressed himself as a warrior, embellishing his visage with tints of red, to show that he was prepared for either war or peace.

As soon as the mudjee monedo arrived, he eyed this strange warrior whom he had never seen before; but he dissembled, as usual, and, with a gentle laugh, said to the widow, "Did I not tell you that some one was staying with you, for I knew your son was too young to hunt."

The widow excused herself by saying that she did

not think it necessary to tell him, inasmuch as he was a manito, and must have known before he asked.

The manito was very pleasant with Monedowa, and after much other discourse, in a gentle-spoken voice, he invited him to the racing-ground, saying it was a manly amusement, that he would have an excellent chance to meet there with other warriors, and that he should himself be pleased to run with him.

Monedowa would have excused himself, saying that he knew nothing of running.

"Why," replied the mudjee monedo, trembling in every limb as he spoke, "don't you see how old I look, while you are young and full of life. We must at least run a little to amuse others."

"Be it so, then," replied Monedowa. "I will oblige you. I will go in the morning."

Pleased with his crafty success, the manito would have now taken his leave, but he was pressed to remain and partake of their hospitality. The meal was immediately prepared. But one dish was used.

Monedowa partook of it first, to show his guest that he need not. fear, saying at the same time, "It is a feast, and as we seldom meet, we must eat all that is placed on the dish, as a mark of gratitude to the Great Spirit for permitting me to kill animals, and for the pleasure of seeing you, and partaking of it with you."

They ate and talked, on this and that, until they had nearly dispatched the meal, when the manito took up the dish and drank off the broth at a breath On setting it down he immediately turned his head and commenced coughing with great violence. The old body in which he had disguised himself was well-nigh shaken in pieces, for he had, as Monedowa expected, swallowed a grain of the birch-bud, and this, which relished to himself as being of the bird nature, greatly distressed the old manito, who partook of the character of an animal, or four-footed thing.

He was at last put to such confusion of face by his constant coughing, that he was enforced to leave, saying, or rather hiccoughing as he left the lodge, that he should look for the young man at the racing-ground in the morning.

When the morning came, Monedowa was early astir, oiling his limbs and enameling his breast and arms with red and blue, resembling the plumage in which he had first appeared to Minda. Upon his brow he placed a tuft of feathers of the same shining tints.

By his invitation his wife, Minda, the mother and her young son, attended Monedowa to the manito's racing-ground.

The lodge of the manito stood upon a high ground, and near it stretched out a long row of other lodges, said to be possessed by wicked kindred of his, who shared in the spoils of his cruelty.

As soon as the young hunter and his party approached, the inmates appeared at their lodge-doors and cried out :

" We are visited."

At this cry, the mudjee monedo came forth and descended with his companions to the starting-post on the plain. From this the course could be seen, winding in a long girdle about the lake ; and as they were now all assembled, the old manito began to speak of the race, belted himself up and pointed to the post, which was an upright pillar of stone.

" But before we start," said the manito, " I wish it to be understood that when men run with me I make a wager, and I expect them to abide by it—life against life."

" Very well—be it so," answered Monedowa. " We shall see whose head is to be dashed against the stone."

" We shall," rejoined the mudjee monedo. " I am very old, but I shall try and make a run."

" Very well," again rejoined Monedowa ; " I hope we shall both stand to our bargain."

" Good !" said the old manito ; and he at the same time cast a sly glance at the young hunter, and rolled his eyes toward where stood the pillar of stone.

" I am ready," said Monedowa.

The starting shout was given, and they set off at high speed, the manito leading, and Monedowa pressing closely after. As he closed upon him, the old manito began to show his power, and changing himself into a fox he passed the young hunter with ease, and went leisurely along.

Monedowa now, with a glance upward, took the shape of the strange bird of red and deep-blue plumage, and with one flight, lighting at some distance ahead of the manito, resumed his mortal shape.

When the mudjee monedo espied his competitor before him, " Whoa ! whoa !" he exclaimed ; " this is strange ;" and he immediately changed himself into a wolf, and sped past Monedowa.

As he galloped by, Monedowa heard a noise from his throat, and he knew that he was still in distress from the birch-bud which he had swallowed at his mother-in-law's lodge.

Monedowa again took wing, and, shooting into the air, he descended suddenly with great swiftness, and took the path far ahead of the old manito.

As he passed the wolf he whispered in his ear :

" My friend, is this the extent of your speed ?"

The manito began to be troubled with bad forebodings, for, on looking ahead, he saw the young hunter in his own manly form, running along at leisure. The mudjee monedo, seeing the necessity of more speed, now passed Monedowa in the shape of a deer.

They were now far around the circle of the lake, and fast closing in upon the starting-post, when

Monedowa, putting on his red and blue plumage, glided along the air and alighted upon the track far in advance.

To overtake him, the old manito assumed the shape of the buffalo ; and he pushed on with such long gallops that he was again the foremost on the course. The buffalo was the last change he could make, and it was in this form that he had most frequently conquered.

The young hunter, once more a bird, in the act of passing the manito, saw his tongue lolling from his mouth with fatigue.

" My friend," said Monedowa, " is this all your speed ?"

The manito made no answer. Monedowa had resumed his character of a hunter, and was within a run of the winning-post, when the wicked manito had nearly overtaken him.

" Bakah ! bakah ! nejee !" he called out to Monedowa ; " stop, my friend, I wish to talk to you."

Monedowa laughed aloud as he replied :

" I will speak to you at the starting-post. When men run with me I make a wager, and I expect them to abide by it—life against life."

One more flight as the blue bird with red wings, and Monedowa was so near to the goal that he could easily reach it in his mortal shape. Shining in beauty, his face lighted up like the sky, with tinted arms and bosom gleaming in the sun, and the parti-colored plume on his brow waving in the wind. Monedowa, cheered by a joyful shout from his own people, leaped to the post.

The manito came on with fear in his face.

" My friend," he said, " spare my life ;" and then added, in a low voice, as if he would not that the others should hear it, " Give me to live." And he began to move off as if the request had been granted.

" As you have done to others," replied Monedowa, " so shall it be done to you."

And seizing the wicked manito, he dashed him against the pillar of stone. His kindred, who were looking on in horror, raised a cry of fear and fled away in a body to some distant land, whence they have never returned.

The widow's family left the scene, and when they had all come out into the open fields, they walked on together until they had reached the fragrant bank and the evergreen wood, where the daughter had first encountered her bird lover.

Monedowa turning to her, said :

" My mother, here we must part. Your daughter and myself must now leave you. The Good Spirit, moved with pity, has allowed me to be your friend. I have done that for which I was sent. I am permitted to take with me the one whom I love. I have found your daughter ever kind, gentle and just. She

14

shall be my companion. The blessing of the Good Spirit be ever with you. Farewell, my mother—my brother, farewell."

While the widow woman was still lost in wonder at these words, Monedowa, and Minda his wife, changed at the same moment, rose into the air, as beautiful birds, clothed in shining colors of red and blue.

They caroled together as they flew, and their songs were happy, and falling, falling, like clear drops, as they rose, and rose, and winged their way far upward, a delicious peace came into the mind of the poor widow woman, and she returned to her lodge deeply thankful at heart for all the goodness that had been shown to her by the Master of Life.

From that day forth she never knew want, and her young son proved a comfort to her lodge, and the tuneful carol of Monedowa and Minda, as it fell from heaven, was a music always, go whither she would, sounding peace and joy in her ear.

XXIV.

BOKWEWA, THE HUMPBACK.

BOKWEWA and his brother lived in a far-off part of the country. By such as had knowledge of them, Bokwewa, the elder, although deformed and feeble of person, was considered a manito, who had assumed the mortal shape; while his younger brother, Kwasynd, manly in appearance, active, and strong, partook of the nature of the present race of beings.

They lived off the path, in a wild, lonesome place, far retired from neighbors, and, undisturbed by cares, they passed their time, content and happy. The days glided by serenely as the river that flowed by their lodge.

Owing to his lack of strength, Bokwewa never engaged in the chase, but gave his attention entirely to the affairs of the lodge. In the long winter evenings he passed the time in telling his brother stories of the giants, spirits, weendigoes, and fairies of the elder age, when they had the exclusive charge of the world. He also at times taught his brother the manner in

which game should be pursued, pointed out to him
the ways of the different beasts and birds of the
chase, and assigned the seasons at which they could
be hunted with most success.

For a while the brother was eager to learn, and
keenly attended to his duties as the provider of the
lodge; but at length he grew weary of their tranquil
life, and began to have a desire to show himself among
men. He became restive in their retirement, and
was seized with a longing to visit remote places.

One day, Kwasynd told his brother that he should
leave him; that he wished to visit the habitations of
men, and to procure a wife.

Bokwewa objected; but his brother overruled all
that he said, and in spite of every remonstrance, he
departed on his travels.

He traveled for a long time. At length he fell in
with the footseps of men. They were moving by
encampments, for he saw, at several spots, the poles
where they had passed. It was winter; and coming to a place where one of their company had died,
he found upon a scaffold, lying at length in the cold
blue air, the body of a beautiful young woman. "She
shall be my wife!" exclaimed Kwasynd.

He lifted her up, and bearing her in his arms, he
returned to his brother. "Brother," he said, "can
not you restore her to life? Oh, do me that favor!"

He looked upon the beautiful female with a longing gaze; but she lay as cold and silent as when he had found her upon the scaffold.

"I will try," said Bokwewa.

These words had been scarcely breathed, when the young woman rose up, opened her eyes, and looked upon Bokwewa with a smile, as if she had known him before.

To Kwasynd she paid no heed whatever; but presently Bokwewa, seeing how she lingered in her gaze upon himself, said to her, "Sister, that is your husband," pointing to Kwasynd.

She listened to his voice, and crossing the lodge, she sat by Kwasynd, and they were man and wife.

For a long time they all lived contentedly together. Bokwewa was very kind to his brother, and sought to render his days happy. He was ever within the lodge, seeking to have it in readiness against the return of Kwasynd from the hunt. And by following his directions, which were those of one deeply skilled in the chase, Kwasynd always succeeded in returning with a good store of meat.

But the charge of the two brothers was greatly lightened by the presence of the spirit-wife; for without labor of the hand, she ordered the lodge, and as she willed, every thing took its place, and was at once in proper array. The wish of her heart seemed to control whatever she looked upon, and it obeyed her desire.

But it was still more to the surprise of her husband Kwasynd that she never partook of food, nor
shared in any way the longings and appetites of a
mortal creature. She had never been seen arranging
her hair, like other females, or at work upon her garments, and yet they were ever seemly, and without
blemish or disorder.

Behold her at any hour, she was ever beautiful,
and she seemed to need no ornament, nor nourish-
ment, nor other aid, to give grace or strength to her
looks.

Kwasynd, when the first wonder of her ways had
passed, payed little heed to her discourse ; he was
engrossed with the hunt, and chose rather to be
abroad, pursuing the wild game, or in the lodge, enjoying its savory spoil, than the society of his spirit-
wife.

But Bokwewa watched closely every word that fell
from her lips, and often forgot, like her, all mortal
appetite and care of the body, in conferring with her,
and noting what she had to say of spirits and fairies,
of stars, and streams that never ceased to flow, and
the delight of the happy hunting-grounds, and the
groves of the blessed.

One day Kwasynd had gone out as usual, and
Bokwewa was sitting in the lodge, on the opposite
side to his brother's wife, when she suddenly exclaimed :

"I must leave you," as a tall young man, whose face was like the sun in its brightness, entered, and taking her by the hand he led her to the door.

She made no resistance, but turning as she left the lodge, she cast upon Bokwewa a smile of kind regard, and was at once, with her companion, gone from his view.

He ran to the door and glanced about. He saw nothing; but looking far off in the sky, he thought that he could discover, at a great distance, a shining track, and the dim figures of two who were vanishing in heaven.

When his brother returned, Bokwewa related all to him exactly as it had happened.

The face of Kwasynd changed, and was dark as the night. For several days he would not taste food. Sometimes he would fall to weeping for a long time, and now only it seemed that he remembered how gentle and beautiful had been the ways of her who was lost. At last he said that he would go in search of her.

Bokwewa tried to dissuade him from it; but he would not be turned aside from his purpose.

"Since you are resolved," said Bokwewa, "listen to my advice. You will have to go South. It is a long distance to the present abiding-place of your wife, and there are so many charms and temptations by the way that I fear you will be led astray and forget your errand. For the people whom you will see in the country through which you have to pass, do nothing but amuse themselves. They are very idle, gay and effeminate, and I fear that they will lead you astray. Your path is beset with dangers. I will mention one or two things which you must be on your guard against.

"In the course of your journey you will come to a large grape-vine lying across your path. You must not even taste its fruit, for it is poisonous. Step over it. It is a snake. You will next come to something that looks like bear's fat, of which you are so fond. Touch it not, or you will be overcome by the soft habits of the idle people. It is frog's eggs. These are snares laid by the way for you."

Kwasynd promised that he would observe the advice and bidding his brother farewell, he set out. After traveling a long time he came to the enchanted grape-vine. It looked so tempting, with its swelling purple clusters, that he forgot his brother's warning, and tasted the fruit. He went on till he came to the frog's eggs. They so much resembled delicious bear's fat that Kwasynd tasted them. He still went on.

At length he came to a wide plain. As he emerged from the forest the sun was falling in the west, and it cast its scarlet and golden shades far over the country. The air was perfectly calm, and the whole prospect had the air of an enchanted land. Fruits and flowers, and delicate blossoms, lured the eye and delighted the senses.

At a distance he beheld a large village, swarming with people, and as he drew near he discovered women beating corn in silver mortars.

When they saw Kwasynd approaching, they cried out:

"Bokwewa's brother has come to see us."

Throngs of men and women, in bright apparel, hurried out to meet him.

He was soon, having already yielded to temptation by the way, overcome by their fair looks and soft speeches, and he was not long afterward seen beating corn with the women, having entirely abandoned all further quest for his lost wife.

Meantime, Bokwewa, alone in the lodge, often musing upon the discourse of the spirit-wife, who was gone, waited patiently his brother's return. After the lapse of several years, when no tidings could be had, he set out in search of him, and he arrived in safety among the soft and idle people of the South. He met the same allurements by the way, and they gathered around him on his coming as they had around his brother Kwasynd; but Bokwewa was proof against their flattery. He only grieved in his heart that any should yield.

He shed tears of pity to see that his brother had laid aside the arms of a hunter, and that he was

14*

beating corn with the women, indifferent to the fate and the fortune of his lost wife.

Bokwewa ascertained that his brother's wife had passed on to a country beyond.

After deliberating for a time, and spending several days in a severe fast, he set out in the direction where he saw that a light shone from the sky.

It was far off, but Bokwewa had a stout heart; and strong in the faith that he was now on the broad path toward the happy land, he pressed forward. For many days he traveled without encountering any thing unusual. And now plains of vast extent, and rich in waving grass, began to pass before his eyes. He saw many beautiful groves, and heard the songs of countless birds.

At length he began to fail in strength for lack of food ; when he suddenly reached a high ground. From this he caught the first glimpse of the other land. But it appeared to be still far off, and all the country between, partly vailed in silvery mists, glittered with lakes and streams of water. As he pressed on, Bokwewa came in sight of innumerable herds of stately deer, moose, and other animals which walked near his path, and they appeared to have no fear of man.

And now again as he wound about in his course, and faced the north once more, he beheld, coming toward him, an immense number of men, women, and children, pressing forward in the direction of the shining land.

In this vast throng Bokwewa beheld persons of every age, from the little infant, the sweet and lovely penaisee, or younger son, to the feeble, gray old man, stooping under the burden of his years.

All whom Bokwewa met, of every name and degree, were heavily laden with pipes, weapons, bows, arrows, kettles and other wares and implements.

One man stopped him, and complained of the weary load he was carrying. Another offered him a kettle; another his bow and arrows; but he declined all, and, free of foot, hastened on.

And now he met women who were carrying their basket-work, and painted paddles, and little boys, with their embellished war-clubs and bows and arrows, the gift of their friends.

With this mighty throng, Bokwewa was borne along for two days and nights, when he arrived at a country so still and shining, and so beautiful in its woods and groves and plains, that he knew it was here that he should find the lost spirit-wife.

He had scarcely entered this fair country, with a sense of home and the return to things familiar strong upon him, when there appeared before him the lost spirit-wife herself, who, taking him by the hand, gave him welcome, saying, " My brother, I am glad to see you. Welcome! welcome! You are now in your native land !"

XXV.

THE CRANE THAT CROSSED THE RIVER.

A FAMOUS hunter who lived in a remote part of
the North had a fair wife and two sons, who
were left in the lodge every day while he went out in
quest of the animals whose flesh was their principal
support.

Game was very abundant in those days, and his labors in the chase were well rewarded. They lived a
long distance from any other lodge, and it was seldom
that they saw any other faces than those of their own
household.

The two sons were still too young to follow their
father in the hunt, and they were in the habit of di-
verting themselves within reach of the lodge.

While thus engaged, they began to take note that
a young man visited the lodge during their father's
absence, and that these visits were constantly renewed.

At length the elder of the two said to his mother:
" My mother, who is this tall young man that

comes here so often during our father's absence?
Does he wish to see him? Shall I tell him when he
comes back this evening?"

"Naubesah, you little fool," said the mother,
"mind your bow and arrows, and do not be afraid to
enter the forest in search of birds and squirrels, with
your little brother. It is not manly to be ever about
the lodge. Nor will you become a warrior if you tell
all the little things that you see and hear to your
father. Say not a word to him."

The boys obeyed, but as they grew older and still
noticed the visits of the stranger, they resolved to
speak again to their mother.

They now told her that they meant to make known
to their father all that they had witnessed, for they
frequently saw this young man passing through the
woods, and he did not walk in the path, nor did he
carry any thing to eat. If he had any message to deliver at their lodge, why did he not give it to their
father? for they had observed that messages were
always addressed to men, and not to women.

When her sons spoke thus to her, the mother was
greatly vexed.

"I will kill you," she said, "if you speak of it."

In fear they for a time held their peace, but still
taking note that the stranger came so often and by
stealth to the lodge, they resolved at last to speak
with their father.

Accordingly one day, when they were out in the woods, learning to follow the chase, they told him all that they had seen.

The face of the father grew dark. He was still for a while, and when at length he looked up—

"It is done!" he said. "Do you, my children, tarry here until the hour of the falling of the sun, then come to the lodge and you will find me."

The father left them at a slow pace, and they remained sporting away their time till the hour for their return had come.

When they reached the lodge the mother was not there. They dared not to ask their father whither she had gone, and from that day forth her name was never spoken again in the lodge.

In course of time the two boys had grown to be men, and although the mother was never more seen in the lodge, in charge of her household tasks, nor on the path in the forest, nor by the river side, she still lingered, ever and ever, near the lodge.

Changed, but the same, with ghastly looks and arms that were withered, she appeared to her sons as they returned from the hunt, in the twilight, in the close of the day.

At night she darkly unlatched the lodge-door and glided in, and bent over them as they sought to sleep. Oftenest it was her bare brow, white, and bony, and bodyless, that they saw floating in the air, and making a mock of them in the wild paths of the forest, or in the midnight darkness of the lodge.

She was a terror to all their lives, and she made every spot where they had seen her, hideous to the living eye; so that after being long buffeted and be-set, they at last resolved, together with their father, now stricken in years, to leave the country.

They began a journey toward the South. After traveling many days along the shore of a great lake, they passed around a craggy bluff, and came upon a scene where there was a rough fall of waters, and a river issuing forth from the lake.

They had no sooner come in sight of this fall of water, than they heard a rolling sound behind them, and looking back, they beheld the skull of a woman rolling along the beach. It seemed to be pursuing them, and it came on with great speed; when, be-hold, from out of the woods hard by, appeared a head-less body, which made for the beach with the utmost dispatch.

The skull too advanced toward it, and when they looked again, lo ! they had united, and were making all haste to come up with the hunter and his two sons. They now might well be in extreme fear, for they knew not how to escape her.

At this moment, one of them looked out and saw a stately crane sitting on a rock in the middle of the rapids. They called out to the bird, "See, grand-

father, we are persecuted. Come and take us across
the falls that we may escape her."

The crane so addressed was of extraordinary size,
and had arrived at a great old age, and, as might be
expected, he sat, when first descried by the two sons,
in a state of profound thought, revolving his long experience of life there in the midst of the most violent eddies.

When he heard himself appealed to, the crane
stretched forth his neck with great deliberation, and
lifting himself slowly by his wings, he flew across to
their assistance.

" Be careful," said the old crane, " that you do
not touch the crown of my head. I am bald from
age and long service, and very tender at that spot.
Should you be so unlucky as to lay a hand upon it, 1
shall not be able to avoid throwing you both in the
rapids."

They paid strict heed to his directions, and were
soon safely landed on the other shore of the river.
He returned and carried the father in the same way;
and then took his place once more where he had been
first seen in the very midst of the eddies of the stream.

But the woman, who had by this time reached the
shore, cried out, " Come, my grandfather, and carry
me over, for I have lost my children, and I am sorely
distressed."

The aged bird obeyed her summons, and flew to

her side. He carefully repeated the warning that she was not to touch the crown of his head; and he was so anxious that she should take it to heart, that he went over it a second and a third time, word by word. He begged her to bear in mind that she should respect his old age, if there was any sense of virtue left in her.

She promised to obey; but they were no sooner fairly embarked in the stream, than she stealthily sought to disregard the warning she had received. Instantly the crane cast her into the rapids, and shook his wings as if to free himself of all acquaintance with her.

" There," said he, as she sunk in the stream, " you would ever do what was forbidden. In life, as you sought those you should have avoided, so now you shall be avoided by those who should seek you. Go, and be henceforth Addum Kum Maig !"

The woman disappeared, was straightway carried by the rapid currents far out into the waters, and in the wide wilderness of shoreless depths, without companion or solace, was lost forever.

The family of the hunter, grateful for his generous help, adopted the bird as their family emblem or mark, and under the guardianship of the Crane that Crossed the River, they prospered, with days of plenty and nights of peace.

XXVI.

WUNZH, THE FATHER OF INDIAN CORN.

IN time past—we can not tell exactly how many, many years ago—a poor Indian was living, with his wife and children, in a beautiful part of the country. He was not only poor, but he had the misfortune to be inexpert in procuring food for his family, and his children were all too young to give him assistance.

Although of a lowly condition and straitened in his circumstances, he was a man of kind and contented disposition. He was always thankful to the Great Spirit for every thing he received. He even stood in the door of his lodge to bless the birds that flew past in the summer evenings; although, if he had been of a complaining temper, he might have repined that they were not rather spread upon the table for his evening meal.

The same gracious and sweet disposition was inherited by his eldest son, who had now arrived at the proper age to undertake the ceremony of the fast, to learn what kind of a spirit would be his guide and guardian through life.

Wunzh, for this was his name, had been an obedient boy from his infancy—pensive, thoughtful, and gentle—so that he was beloved by the whole family. As soon as the first buds of spring appeared, and the delicious fragrance of the young year began to sweeten the air, his father, with the help of his younger brothers, built for Wunzh the customary little lodge, at a retired spot at some distance from their own, where he would not be disturbed during the solemn rite.

To prepare himself, Wunzh sought to clear his heart of every evil thought, and to think of nothing that was not good, and beautiful, and kindly.

That he might store his mind with pleasant ideas for his dreams, for the first few days he amused himself by walking in the woods and over the mountains, examining the early plants and flowers.

As he rambled far and wide, through the wild country, he felt a strong desire to know how the plants and herbs and berries grew, without any aid from man, and why it was that some kinds were good to eat, and that others were possessed of medicinal or poisonous power.

After he had become too languid to walk about, and confined himself strictly to the lodge, he recalled these thoughts, and turning them in his mind, he wished he could dream of something that would prove a benefit to his father and family, and to all others of his fellow-creatures.

"True," thought Wunzh, "the Great Spirit made all things, and it is to him that we owe our lives. Could he not make it easier for us to get our food, than by hunting animals and taking fish? I must try to find this out in my visions."

On the third day Wunzh became weak and faint, and kept his bed. Suddenly he fancied, as he lay thus, that a bright light came in at the lodge door, and ere he was aware, he saw a handsome young man, with a complexion of the softest and purest white, coming down from the sky, and advancing toward him.

The beautiful stranger was richly and gayly dressed, having on a great many garments of green and yellow colors, but differing in their deeper or lighter shades. He had a plume of waving feathers on his head, and all his motions were graceful, and reminded Wunzh of the deep green of the summer grass, and the clear amber of the summer sky, and the gentle blowing of the summer wind. Beautiful as the stranger was, he paused on a little mound of earth, just before the door of the lodge.

"I am sent to you, my friend," said this celestial visitor, in a voice most soft and musical to listen to, "I am sent to you by that Great Spirit who made all things in the sky, and on the earth. He has seen and knows your motives in fasting. He sees that it is from a kind and benevolent wish to do good to your people, and to procure a benefit for them ; that you do not seek for strength in war, or the praise of the men of the bloody hand. I am sent to instruct you and to show you how you can do your kindred good."

He then told the young man to arise, and to prepare to wrestle with him, as it was only by this means that he could hope to succeed in his wishes.

Wunzh knew how weak he was from fasting, but the voice of the stranger was cheery, and put such a courage in his heart, that he promptly sprang up, determined to die rather than fail. Brave Wunzh! if you ever accomplish any thing, it will be through the power of the resolve that spake within you at that moment.

He began the trial, and after a long-sustained struggle he was almost overpowered, when the beautiful stranger said :

" My friend, it is enough for once, I will come again to try you ;" and smiling on him, he returned through the air in the same direction in which he had come.

The next day, although he saw how sweetly the wild-flowers bloomed upon the slopes, and the birds warbled from the woodland, he longed to see the celestial visitor, and to hear his voice.

To his great joy he reappeared at the same hour, toward the going down of the sun, and re-challenged Wunzh to a trial of strength.

The brave Wunzh felt that his strength of body was even less than on the day before, but the courage of his mind seemed to grow. Observing this, and how Wunzh put his whole heart in the struggle, the stranger again spoke to him in the words he used before, adding :

"To-morrow will be your last trial. Be strong, my friend, for this is the only way in which you can overcome me and obtain the boon you seek."

The light which shone after him as he left Wunzh was brighter than before.

On the third day he came again and renewed the struggle. Very faint in body was poor Wunzh, but he was stronger at heart than ever, and determined to prevail now or perish. He put forth his utmost powers, and after a contest more severe than either of the others, the stranger ceased his efforts, and declared himself conquered.

For the first time he entered Wunzh's little fasting-lodge, and sitting down beside the youth, he began to deliver his instructions to him and to inform him in what manner he should proceed to take advantage of his victory.

"You have won your desire of the Great Spirit," said the beautiful stranger. "You have wrestled manfully. To-morrow will be the seventh day of your fasting. Your father will give you food to strengthen you, and as it is the last day of trial you will prevail. I know this, and now tell you what you must do to benefit your family and your people. To-morrow," he repeated, " I shall meet you and wrestle with you for the last time. As soon as you have prevailed against me, you will strip off my garments and throw me down, clean the earth of roots and weeds, make it soft, and bury me in the spot. When you have done this, leave my body in the earth, and do not disturb it, but come at times to visit the place, to see whether I have come to life, and above all be careful to never let the grass or weeds grow upon my grave. Once a month cover me with fresh earth. If you follow these my instructions you will accomplish your object of doing good to your fellow-creatures by teaching them the knowledge I now teach you."

He then shook Wunzh by the hand and disappeared, but he was gone so soon that Wunzh could not tell what direction he took.

In the morning, Wunzh's father came to his lodge with some slight refreshments, saying :

" My son, you have fasted long enough. If the Great Spirit will favor you, he will do it now. It is seven days since you have tasted food, and you must not sacrifice your life. The Master of Life does not require that."

" My father," replied Wunzh, " wait till the sun goes down. I have a particular reason for extending my fast to that hour."

" Very well," said the old man, " I shall wait till the hour arrives, and you shall be inclined to eat."

At his usual hour of appearing, the beautiful sky-visitor returned, and the trial of strength was renewed. Although he had not availed himself of his father's offer of food, Wunzh felt that new strength had been given him. His heart was mighty within him to achieve some great purpose. Courage was like the eagle that spreads his wings within the tree-top for a great flight, within the bosom of the brave Wunzh.

He grasped his angel challenger with supernatural strength, threw him down, and, mindful of his own instructions, tore from him his beautiful garments and plume, and finding him dead, he immediately buried him on the spot, using all the precautions he had been told of, and very confident was Wunzh, all the time, that his friend would again come to life.

Wunzh now returned to his father's lodge, where he was warmly welcomed, for as it had been appointed to him during the days of his fasting to walk apart with Heaven, he was not permitted to see any human face save that of his father, the representative to the little household upon earth of the Good Father who is in Heaven.

Wunzh partook sparingly of the meal that had been prepared for him, and once more mingled in the cares and sports of the family. But he never for a moment forgot the grave of his friend. He carefully visited it throughout the spring, and weeded

out the grass, and kept the ground in a soft and pli-
ant state ; and sometimes, when the brave Wunzh
thought of his friend that was gone from his sight,
he dropped a tear upon the earth where he lay.
Watching and tending, and moistening the earth
with his tears, it was not long before Wunzh saw the
tops of green plumes coming through the ground ;
and the more faithful he was in obeying his instructions in keeping the ground in order, and in cherish-
ing the memory of his departed friend, the faster
they grew. He was, however, careful to conceal the
charge of the earth which he had from his father.

Days and weeks had passed in this way ; the summer was drawing toward a close, when one day, after
a long absence in hunting, Wunzh invited his father
to follow him to the quiet and lonesome spot of his
former fast.

The little fasting-lodge had been removed, and the
weeds kept from growing on the circle where it had
stood ; but in its place rose a tall and graceful plant,
surmounted with nodding plumes and stately leaves,
and golden clusters. There was in its aspect and
bearing the deep green of the summer grass, the clear
amber of the summer sky, and the gentle blowing of
the summer wind.

" It is my friend !" shouted Wunzh, " it is the
friend of all mankind. It is Mondawmin : it is our
Indian Corn ! We need no longer rely on hunting
15

alone, for as long as this gift is cherished and taken care of, the ground itself will give us a living."

He then pulled an ear.

"See, my father," said he, "this is what I fasted for. The Great Spirit has listened to my voice, and sent us something new, and henceforth our people will not alone depend upon the chase or upon the waters."

Wunzh then communicated to his father the instructions given to him by the stranger. He told him that the broad husks must be torn away, as he had pulled off the garments in his wrestling, and having done this, he directed him how the ear must be held before the fire till the outer skin became brown—as the complexion of his angel friend had been tinted by the sun—while all the milk was retained in the grain.

The whole family, in high spirits, and deeply grateful to the Merciful Master who gave it, assisted in a feast on the newly-grown ears of corn.

So came that mighty blessing into the world, and we owe all of those beautiful fields of healthful grain to the dream of the brave boy Wunzh.

THE END.

NEW BOOKS

FOR THE

YOUNG FOLKS.

I. THE WONDER WORLD. Stories from the French, German, Hungarian, Irish, Russian, Turkish, Hindostanee, Chinese, Swedish, Italian and Japanese. Collected and translated by MARIA PABKE and MARGERY DEANE. With illustrations by LUCY G. MORSE. 8vo, cloth extra.

II. THE ENCHANTED MOCCASINS and OTHER LEGENDS of the AMER'CAN INDIANS. Compiled from original sources by CORNELIUS MATHEUS. 8vo, illustrated, cloth extra.

III. PATSY. By LEORA B. ROBINSON Uniform with "The House with Spectacles." Square 16mo, cloth extra, $1.25.

IV. SIX SINNERS. By CAMPBELL WHEATON, uniform with "The House with Spectacles." Square 16mo, cloth extra, $1.25.

V. THE SIGNAL BOYS; or, CAPT. SAM'S COMPANY. By GEO. CARY EGGLESTON. Vol. III. of "The Big Brother" Series. With illustrations. 8vo, cloth extra, $1.50.

VI. THE WINGS OF COURAGE. Stories for American Boys and Girls, adapted from the French, by MARIE E. FIELD. With illustrations by LUCY G. MORSE. Square 16mo, cloth extra, $1.25.

VII. THE CHILDREN'S PARADISE. By KATHERINE B. ZEREGA. With illustrations by LUCY G. MORSE. Square 16mo, cloth extra, $1.25.

"The writer combines a true poetical spirit with admirable good humor, and good taste."—*N. Y. Tribune.*

FASCINATING BOOKS FOR YOUNG PEOPLE.

Moonfolk: A True Account of the Home of the Fairy Tales. By Jane G. Austin. Illustrated by 65 designs drawn and engraved on wood by W. J. Linton. 8vo : cloth extra, - - - - $1 75
" The most fascinating juvenile since ' Alice in Wonderland.' "—*Christian Union.*

History of My Friends; or, Home Life with Animals. By A. Achard. Translated from the French. With 12 full page illustrations. 12mo : cloth extra, $1 50

The Girlhood of Shakespeare's Heroines: in a series of Tales. By Mary Cowden Clarke. Large 12mo ; illustrated. 2 vols. in box (sold separately), $4 00
" Her imagination, retracing of influence and development is symmetrical, consistent and skillful, and she has woven her characters into charming stories."—*N. Y. Evening Mail.*

The Shakespeare Treasury of Wisdom and Knowledge. By Chas. W. Stearns, M.D. In an elegant volume, tinted paper. Cloth extra, - - - $2 00
" Full of valuable ideas."—*Boston Commonwealth.*
" The scholar and student will find Dr. Stearn's volume an invaluable guide and help."—*Providence Journal.*

Poetry for Home and School. Edited by Anna C. Brackett and Ida M. Eliot. A selection of short pieces selected from the best standard English and American Authors. Square 16mo : cloth, - $1 25
" An idea carried out with discrimination and intelligence."—*Nation.*
" This book deserves the attention of every school committee, and parents will search long without finding so good a collection for fireside reading."—*Christian Union.*

The Silver Treasury. The Holiday Edition of Poetry for Home and School. Cloth, extra gilt, illustrated, with side stamp in silver, - - $1 75
The Book is divided in two parts : the first containing poems designed for children from six to ten years of age; in the second are more serious and thoughtful poems for older children.
" An exquisite little gift-book."

Wonders of the Deep. By M. Schele De Vere, Professor in the University of Virginia. Third Edition. 12mo : cloth, illustrated, $1 50 ; gilt, $1 75
" One of the freshest, most scientific, and at the same time most popular and delightful books of the kind we have ever read."—*St. John's Telegraph.*

G. P. PUTNAM'S SONS,

182 Fifth Ave., New York.

NEW BOOKS.

The Gold of Chickaree. By SUSAN and ANNA WARNER, authors of " The Wide,Wide World," " Wych Hazel," etc. Large 12mo, cloth extra, $1.75

Of "Wych Hazel," the *Boston Traveller* says—"We have not the faintest hesitation in placing this work above anything the authors have given us, and furthermore in placing it among the very strongest novels in character development which have been written during the past two years.

Wych Hazel. By SUSAN AND ANNA WARNER. 12mo, cloth, $2.

" The whole structure of the story is symmetrical and harmonious—one of the best written and most entertaining recently sent out by any of the favorites of the novel reading public."—*Albany Journal.*

" There is a realism in the characters and scenes of the story, which is a prime condition of success in books of this kind. It can hardly fail to be read by thousands and be very popular.—*N. Y. Evangelist.*

The Select British Essayists. A Series planned to consist of half a dozen volumes, comprising the Representative Papers of *The Spectator, Tatler, Guardian, Rambler, Lounger, Mirror, Looker-On,* etc., etc. Edited, with Introduction and Biographical Sketches of the Authors, by JOHN HABBERTON.

Vol. I.—The Spectator. BY ADDISON and STEELE. Square 16mo, beautifully printed, and tastefully bound in cloth extra, $1.25.

This Series has been planned to preserve, and to present in a form at once attractive and economical, the permanently valuable portions of those standard productions of the Essayists, which, as well for the perfection of their English style, as for the sterling worth of their matter, are deservedly perennial.

Vol. II. **Sir Roger de Coverly Papers.** From *The Spectator.* One volume, 16mo, $1.00.

" Mr. Habberton has given us a truly readable and delightful selection from a series of volumes that ought possibly never to go out of fashion, but which by the reason of their length and slightly antiquated form, there is danger of our overlooking."—*Liberal Christian.*

Poetry for Home and School. A selection of short pieces selected from the best standard English and American authors. Edited by ANNA C. BRACKETT and IDA M. ELIOT. Square 16mo. Cloth, pp. 320., $1.25. Holiday Edition of the same.

The Silver Treasury of Poetry for House and School. With steel plates, full gilt, $1.75.

" An idea carried out with discrimination and intelligence."—*Nation.*

"It is as fresh and bright as a beautiful spring morning."—*Wilmington Review.*

"An easier or more readable book could hardly be placed upon the centre table."—*Yale Lit.*

"For its purpose * * unqualifiedly the best collection that has been made."—*Eclectic Magazine.*

"No more charming and refining collection of poetry can be put in the hands of children."—*New Bedford Mercury.*

The Plains of the Great West and their Inhabitants. A vivid and picturesque description of the Western Plains of the American Continent, including accounts of the game, a careful topographical record, notes of emigration, etc., etc., and an exhaustive account of the life and habits of the Indians (both the "reserved" and the "unreserved,") their customs in fighting, hunting, marriage, death, clothing, religious beliefs and rites, etc., etc., with some suggestions for the treatment of the Indian question.

By RICHARD IRVING DODGE, Colonel in the U. S. Army. One large octavo volume, very fully illustrated. 8vo, cloth, $4.

G. P. PUTNAM'S SONS.

182 Fifth Avenue, New York.

READABLE BOOKS

FOR ALL SEASONS.

I. THE DEVIL PUZZLERS, AND OTHER STUDIES.
  By F. B. PERKINS. Square 16mo, with frontispiece. Paper, 50 cts.; cloth, $1.00.

II. HIS GRANDMOTHERS:
  A ROMANCE OF REAL LIFE.
  By a New Writer. Square 16mo, with frontispiece. Paper, 50 cts.; cloth, $1.00.

III. THE JOHNSON MANOR:
  A TALE OF NEW YORK IN OLDEN TIME.
  By JAMES KENT. Square 12mo, cloth extra, $1.50.

IV. HER SACRIFICE:
  A STORY OF ENGLISH LIFE.
  By X. 8vo, paper, 75 cts.; cloth, $1.25.

V. DIANA.
  By SUSAN WARNER. Author of "The Wide, Wide World," "Wych-Hazel," etc. (*In Press.*)

VI. MY THREE CONVERSATIONS WITH MISS CHESTER.
  By F. B. PERKINS. No. I. of "TALES FOR TRAVELLERS." Square 16mo, paper, 25 cts.

VII. SEA STORIES:
  Containing "Barney O'Reirdon, the Navigator," "The Sunken Rock,' "MS Found in a Bottle," "The Irish Pilot," "The Loss of the Wager," "Why the Sea is Salt," etc. 12mo, paper, 50 cts.

VIII. STORIES FOR THE HOME CIRCLE:
  Containing "A Game of Chess with Napoleon," "The Purloined Letter," "The Left Hand Glove," "The Mysterious Salute," "Catching a Resurrectionist," etc. 12mo, paper, 50 cts.